♘

Look for other *SHOW STRIDES* books:

#1 School Horses and Show Ponies

#2 Confidence Comeback

#3 Moving Up and Moving On

#4 Testing Friendships

5
· SHOW STRIDES ·
Packer Pressure

Series created by
Rennie Dyball

Published by
The Plaid Horse

Copyright © 2022 by Piper Klemm
The Plaid Horse, Canton, New York

Library of Congress Control Number: 2022915469
Show Strides: Packer Pressure / Piper Klemm
Text by Rennie Dyball
Illustrations © 2022 by The Plaid Horse

ISBN: 978-1-7329632-5-2

Printed in the United States of America
First Printing

Silver Lake Press
www.silverlakepress.net / (781) 293-2276

MAP OF
QUINCE OAKS

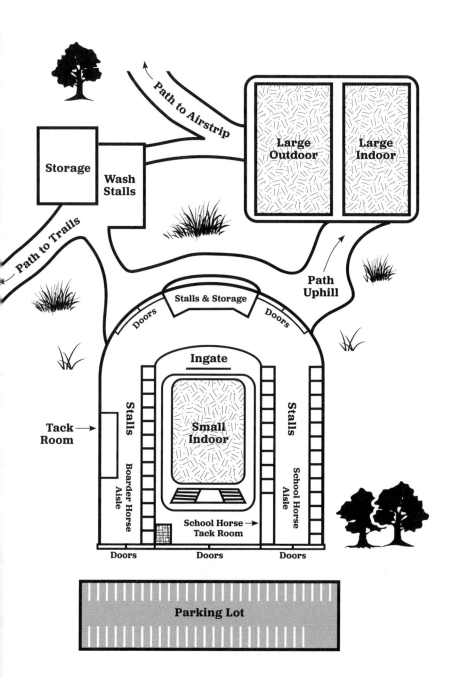

· CHAPTER 1 ·

"I have bad news and I have good news," said Ryan. "Actually, make that *very* good news."

Tally looked up at her trainer from inside one of the school pony's stalls. It was the day after Halloween, but the horses were still in a spooky state of mind. High winds outside had been rattling the windows in the indoor ring—and the horses and ponies in the lesson as well. Tally had been asked to hop off her horse and onto the most nervous pony to end the animal's ride on a confident note. She felt really proud whenever someone trusted her to put in a good ride.

"I guess you should get the bad news out of the way first, right?" Tally said, giving the pony's leg one more swipe with her soft brush.

Ryan's expression sank a bit. Tally held her breath.

"I have a kid who's going to lease Obie for a year," said Ryan. "Starting this month."

Tally felt herself deflate. She had been riding Obie as a project horse for Ryan, and even took him to his very first show. Sensitive and sweet—but super lazy—Obie had really progressed with Tally over several months at Field Ridge, Ryan's show barn. The horse had been a great teacher for her, too. If you didn't ask correctly, Obie simply wouldn't do what you wanted.

"Wow, okay. Well, I knew he'd find his own person, I just didn't realize it would be so fast," said Tally. As a catch-rider for her trainer, she understood that the ponies and horses Ryan paired her with would only be hers until they were sold or leased. But it still stung each time she found herself without a regular ride.

"Don't you want to hear the good news now?" Ryan asked, breaking into a small smile.

"Oh, right! Yes, the good news," Tally answered with a laugh. "What is it?"

"Walk with me," Ryan said. He was full-on grinning now.

Tally latched the pony's stall door behind her and followed Ryan around to the other side of the barn.

Quince Oaks was an expansive, horseshoe-shaped facility, with school horses on one aisle for the lesson program, and Ryan McNeil's private hunter-jumper operation, Field Ridge, on the other. Tally rode the "schoolies" exclusively for many years and still cared for them in her role as a working student, so she felt equally at home on both sides of the barn.

They rounded the corner to the Field Ridge aisle, and Ryan stopped in front of stall Four.

"You know Cameron, right?" asked Ryan, gesturing to the horse inside.

"Sure," said Tally, reaching up to stroke Cam's face as he stuck his head out to greet them. A stunning bay roan with a white blaze and four white stockings, Cam was hard to miss.

"*Wellllll...*" said Ryan, drawing the word out as if to prolong the wait for his news.

"Yes?" Tally asked with a grin of her own.

"Cam's owner, Pia, is in Europe for work all this month, and likely into December as well. She shows Cam in the Adult Amateur Hunters. She needs him to stay in work for them to show this winter when she returns."

Tally searched Ryan's face for a hint about how she fit into the equation. *This couldn't mean that...*

"Pia wants to give you Cam for the month or two that she's away. You can ride him and show him as much as you want."

Tally shook her head in disbelief. "Me? Why?"

"Because of all your hard work," Ryan said, his tone definitive. "Pia noticed how much time you put into Obie, and with Goose before him. She told me she wants you to have the ride on Cam and enjoy him. She also knows how well you take care of the horses you ride, and she wants him to be loved and in good hands until she returns.

Tally still couldn't wrap her head around the idea of a seasoned show horse being hers, even temporarily. "Thank you! Oh my gosh, I can't believe this. I can *show* him, too?"

"Yup," Ryan said with a laugh. "You can walk right into the Low Children's hunters on this one. You'll have a blast. He's such a good boy...wins a lot too. Always an added bonus, right?"

Tally stared at Cam, who was now nosing around the hay in the corner of the stall. *Was this actually real?*

☍

"I still can't believe this, but it all sounds great," said Tally. "Can I thank Pia? Is she coming out today?"

"She left for Europe a couple of days ago," said Ryan. "But I'll give you her email address so you can write her a note. You're going to love this horse, Tal. And you've earned it."

CHAPTER 2

"Cameron? Like *the* Cameron? The barn favorite who wins everything and everyone loves?"

"Yup," said Tally, laughing at her friend's wide-eyed expression.

"Tally, this is huge!" said Mac, wrapping her friend up in a hug. Mac's pony, Joey, nudged the girls with his nose, eager to get in on the celebration.

"I know," said Tally, bending down to unwrap one of Joey's polos alongside her friend. "I've never ridden a horse this experienced. It's going to be weird!"

"It's going to be *awesome*," Mac corrected her. Mackenzie (Mac) Bennett was Tally's best friend at the barn. At this point, probably her best friend, period. Mac had arrived about a year ago with Joey, a.k.a. Smoke Hill Jet Set, her partner in the Medium

Pony Hunter division. When the girls first met, Tally knew next to nothing about the A circuit, having ridden only in the lesson program and at the barn's in-house schooling shows. Now, Tally had competed several times at rated shows off the property, spectated at Devon and Pony Finals, and spent many sleepovers with Mac watching live streams and replays of the biggest shows in the country. There was nothing she loved more than immersing herself in the world of horses and showing.

"How was your lesson?" Tally asked.

"Great. Really great, actually," Mac said, rubbing her chestnut pony's neck. Joey licked Mac's hand, in case a treat should materialize there. "But Ryan said he wanted to meet with me and my parents tonight, so I'm not sure what that's about. How was your lesson?"

"It was good, I rode Obie and then I got on Toots because he was being extra spooky for his rider. I wish I'd known it was my last ride on Obie, though...Ryan has a kid who's going to lease him. I wish I could have explained to him what's happening. Or something..." Tally paused. "That sounds stupid right?"

Mac shook her head no, her expression serious.

"I'm so excited for Cam, but it's still a little hard to move on. Remember when I cried in the porta-potties after I saw Goose at a show?" Goose was a green small pony that Tally helped bring along for Ryan. He got sold over the summer and it wasn't easy seeing him with his new owner at a show back in September.

"Aw, Tal, that's what makes you so good at this, though. You really love them," said Mac. "And they love you, too."

"I hope so," Tally said with a sigh. "And it's great for Obie to have a person of his own. Ryan told me it's one of his newer students who's going to show in the Long Stirrup."

A gust of wind whipped down the aisle. Joey raised his head on the cross ties and Mac jogged for the doorway.

"Hold on, everybody!" she called to the horses before sliding the big, heavy door closed. The mood on the aisle calmed down within seconds.

Tally and Mac were putting their tack away when Brenna, the Oaks barn manager, rounded the corner.

"Oh good, you're all tucked in over here," Brenna said.

"Nobody was thrilled with that wind so I just closed the big doors. Hope that's okay," said Mac.

"Totally, thank you," Brenna replied. "Everyone's staying in for the night. Gusts are going to get up to forty miles per hour and the temperature is dropping, too. You can put the stable blankets on them, girls."

Mac disappeared into the tack room and Tally slipped into Cam's stall. He was already wearing his blanket for the night but she couldn't resist a quick goodbye.

"Hi, sweet boy," she said. Cam turned to face her. His eyes were big and soft. Tally could feel his kindness, just looking at him.

"I can't believe I get to ride you for a month. Might even be two," she said, stroking the horse's neck. Cam wasn't super tall—probably a bit under 16 hands, Tally guessed—but he was big through his body. She'd seen him around the barn, of course, but she had very little idea of what he'd be like to ride.

Down the aisle, both Tally and Cam heard the unmistakable *swish* of grain being dropped into a bucket. It was dinner time. Cam turned away from Tally and stuck his nose in the feed bucket in the far corner of his stall.

"Well, it's not there yet, buddy," Tally said laughing. "Are you reminding us where your dinner should go?"

Cam faced her again. Something about his expression, those huge, soft eyes, filled Tally with affection. She didn't even know this horse yet, but she already felt a fondness for him. Cam nickered and turned his head toward the sound of the feeding crew, heading in his direction.

"Have a good dinner, Cam," Tally said, giving him one more pat before heading home.

· CHAPTER 3 ·

The next day after school, Tally got to the barn a little earlier than usual to take her time grooming Cam and getting to know him on the ground. As it turned out, she was *really* early, and the horse was fully groomed well before Tally needed to be ready for the lesson. She was putting him back in his stall when Mac walked up to Cam's doorway.

"Hey, so...I think I have some big news, too," Mac said. She didn't really sound much like herself.

"You do?" Tally asked, securing the door behind her.

Mac nodded. She looked uncomfortable and Tally's stomach dropped a little. The girls had been through a misunderstanding and a lot of hurt feelings over the summer. Not talking to her best friend every day had been so hard on Tally, and now she was worried something had come up again.

"What's wrong?" she asked Mac, following her down the aisle.

"Nothing wrong, really. I think I'm more surprised than anything." Mac took a deep breath. "Ryan thinks I'm ready to move up from the Medium Ponies with Joey. He wants me to move up to the Large Ponies."

"Mac! That *is* big news," Tally said. She forgot all about her worries that Mac's news had anything to do with her.

"I know. I just can't really imagine Joey not being mine anymore, you know?" The girls had arrived at the bleachers that overlooked the small indoor at the front of the barn. Mac sat down and Tally sat next to her. One of Ryan's boarders was flatting her horse at the far end of the ring. Nicole, an instructor for the riding school, was on the other end, talking a student through her approach to a cross-rail.

"So...you'd be selling him?" Tally asked.

"I'm not sure yet," Mac told her. "Ryan is starting to look for larges for me right away, but I don't think my parents would ever let me have two ponies at once. Listen, moving up to the Large Ponies and horse shopping, it's all a good thing, I know that, and I'm sorry to complain. I know how much you want a horse of your own."

Tally shook her head and scooted a little closer to her friend. "It's okay. I know how sad it is to move on from a ride, but moving on from a pony who's been yours for years sounds even harder."

Both girls gazed out on the lesson. Gelati, a leopard Appaloosa pony, was trotting over the small jump while her rider grabbed a handful of her long, thick mane. The little rider's huge smile was contagious—it made Mac smile, too.

"Remember those days?" she said.

Tally nodded. It had only been about a year since she'd moved up from the lesson program herself. She loved the years she spent in the riding school, but riding horses and ponies for Ryan was special in a whole new way.

CHAPTER 4

"More trot, Tally. He's trying to bait you into less. You always need *more* on this horse. Leg on! More impulsion!" Ryan called out from the center of the small indoor ring. "That's it. Good. Maintain *that* trot."

Tally felt like giggling, her new horse was so cool. Cameron was truly a "been there, done that" adult hunter—a beautiful mover with a calm, kind disposition. From the moment they picked up the trot, she could feel that he was special. He felt lofty and light as he sprung into the trot from behind. Ryan told her that Cam had really good breeding, which was part of the reason he was still going strong in a three-foot division at 18 years old. That, paired with being relatively low-mileage (he hadn't jumped and competed over the years nearly as much as other

18-year-old show horses), made Cameron a perfect veteran teacher.

"Do you feel the difference?" Ryan asked. Tally nodded.

"He's carrying *you* now, so just keep a nice soft leg. If you need more impulsion, more leg. A little nudge with your spur should do it. Mac, that's great on this new pony, just make sure you're not getting behind the motion. Keep a forward angle in your hip...perfect. Maggie, start Joey off on a serpentine."

Tally concentrated on asking Cam to turn with her legs, using the shifting motion with her hands that Ryan had shown her on Obie. Ryan told her that shifting her hands to the inside through the turns would translate to Cam as well, as both horses had soft mouths and preferred very light contact.

Now that Tally had Cam trotting forward, they were catching up to Joey and Maggie in front of them. Tally circled to make some more room. At the far end of the ring, Mac was riding a large pony that Ryan had brought in on trial. The new pony was fancy as could be—a reddish bay with a jet-black mane and tail, with not a spot of white on his body.

After another length of the ring on the serpentine, Ryan asked the girls to walk and come into the middle. He stepped down from his director's chair, embroidered on the back with "Field Ridge."

"So, lots of new things happening, right?" Ryan asked, putting a hand on Joey's forehead. The chestnut pony closed his eyes and sighed.

"Maggie, we'll start trying horses and ponies this weekend," he said. Maggie had done a short-term lease on Joey over the summer while Mac was laid up with a broken wrist from a mounting accident. "You'll keep riding Joey until we find you a horse. Or until we find someone to lease Joey, whichever comes first."

So Joey *wasn't* getting sold! Tally shot a glance at Mac, who gave Tally a little nod and a smile.

Ryan continued: "Tally's got the ride on our resident unicorn, Cam. Isn't he cool, Tal?"

Tally nodded. "I love him already and we haven't even cantered yet."

"And Mac, how are you liking Sparkles?"

Maggie stifled a giggle.

"I know, I know, the name makes him sound like a cartoon pony," Ryan said. "Mac, head out to the rail and pick up your right lead canter. Tally, Mags, space yourselves out and go canter, too. We're in this small ring for a few days while they replace the footing up in the big indoor. Good practice for under saddle classes and finding your own space."

Tally walked Cam past a cross-rail on the quarter line and signaled him to pick up his right lead. He picked up the left. She slowed the horse back down to a trot and put her inside leg on more firmly to make sure he knew what she was asking him to do. He promptly stepped back into the left lead canter again.

"Tally, I forgot to tell you. He's weird about his right lead. And he's 18, so we're not going to change that now. You have to sort of insinuate, or pretend, like you're turning to the right. Try again."

Tally felt her face flush. She had the barn unicorn and she couldn't even get him to pick up his right lead.

After yet another failed attempt, Tally turned her head to the right and shifted her hands like they were turning, then cued Cam for the right lead. He picked it right up.

"That's it! This will get easier with time. He's just funny about it," said Ryan. "Slow down a little Mac...

good. Count your rhythm, don't let Sparkles dictate it for you. Maggie, catch this little X your next time around. Girls, follow Maggie."

Cam's canter was just as smooth and dreamy as his trot, and as they approached the X, Tally felt super-relaxed. Ryan had always told her to simply count her rhythm and not to *look* for a distance. That had been easier said than done on some of the trickier projects she'd ridden. On Cam, it felt natural for Tally just to ride the rhythm and wait for the jump to come to her.

After the lesson was done, the girls lined up on the Field Ridge aisle cross ties to untack and clean up the horses. Tally remembered the maintenance it took to keep white legs clean from her days riding Goose. She brought her grooming box over to restore Cam's legs to their original color.

"I can't believe you're riding a pony named Sparkles," Maggie teased Mac as the girls brushed their ponies.

"Oh, his show name is even better," Mac said, scratching the bay pony's withers.

Tally and Maggie looked at her expectantly.

"*Sparklepants.*" Mac couldn't help laughing and shaking her head.

"No!" said Maggie.

"Yup. Actually, when we went to try him, Ryan thought his show name was Mister Sparklepants, so this is a bit more subtle."

"He looks like a Sparklepants," said Tally. The pony was almost impossibly cute. He had a slightly dished face, a sweet expression, and a trot that Tally could tell would win a lot of hack classes. "You guys looked great together," she added to Mac. "How did you like him?"

"I was starting to think I could only ride Joey," Mac said with a shrug. "It's only been two rides so far on Sparkles, but I think this might work. And Tally, you're killing it on Cam already."

"He makes it easy," Tally said, wrapping up Cam's neck in a hug. "What about you, Maggie? Are you going to look at ponies or horses?"

"I'm not really sure yet. Ryan said he was going to have me try whatever seems like a good fit, so I bet it could be a horse or a pony," said Maggie.

"He can be a little secretive like that," Mac chimed in. "But, as he likes to tell me, there's always a plan!"

· CHAPTER 5 ·

Tally tapped her pen against the edge of her history book as a group of eighth-grade girls gossiped loudly about who was going to the winter dance with whom. It was impossible to study in her blended-grade study hall period.

"Hey," someone whispered from the row in front her.

Tally looked up to see Jacob Viston, a friend from the barn and a seventh grader at her school, Susan B. Anthony West.

"The sub has earbuds in, look," he said, nodding in the direction of the teacher at the front of the classroom, intently reading a magazine. "Quality education right here, huh?"

Tally laughed. "I just read the same paragraph three times. I can't concentrate now that I know that *Aubrey* got asked to the dance by *two* eighth graders!"

One of the gossipers glanced in her direction.

"Any news on Carlo?" Tally asked Jacob.

"Not yet," he said. Jacob's jumper, Carlo, had been injured and wasn't staying sound, so Jacob's mom sent him to be rehabbed. "I don't have a great feeling about it, though. We haven't heard much from the trainer who's working with him."

"That's sad," said Tally.

"It is, but whatever happens I just want him to be happy and live out the best life possible, you know? Whenever I visit him over at the other farm he seems thrilled to run around the field with his little donkey friend, so I don't think he's missing the jumper life too much!"

The substitute teacher shushed the class. Both Tally and Jacob returned to their work for a bit. When the other kids started their whispered conversations back up, Jacob turned back around in his blue plastic chair.

"So, who have you been riding at Oaks?" Tally asked in a whisper.

"Mostly Sweetie, still," said Jacob. "We did the Halloween schooling show and won the medal!"

"That's awesome," Tally said, smiling at the memory of her favorite school horse.

"What about you? Are you still riding Obie?"

Tally shook her head no. "He just got leased to a newer kid at the barn. But I get to ride this boarder's horse Cameron for all of this month, and maybe December. Oh, shoot, that reminds me, I need to email her."

"I've seen Cameron go, he's awesome," said Jacob.

This horse was practically famous, Tally thought to herself.

"I used to see him at the shows before I came to Oaks," continued Jacob. "He's like a mini Clydesdale with those markings but he moves like a fancy show horse."

The substitute teacher pushed his chair back, sending a shrill squeak through the room. Kids covered their ears and everyone got quiet.

"I tried to treat you all like adults and get the chatter out of your systems, but no one seems to be stopping, so I have to treat you like children. Everyone sit down right now, no more talking for the rest of the period," he said.

There were some groans and some whispers, but within moments, the room was quiet. Study hall was designated for whatever work students saw fit to complete. Tally figured the email to Cam's owner counted as work. She took her laptop out of her backpack and opened a blank page to draft the note.

"Dear Pia … Hi Pia … Dear Ms. …."

Tally realized she didn't even know Pia's last name. The barn was funny like that. Everyone was on a first name basis, whether you were a kid, an adult, or somewhere in between. She decided to ask Ryan how to address Pia and moved on to the note itself.

> *"Thank you so much for thinking of me to ride Cameron while you are out of the country. I am so excited! Excited is not really a big enough word for it. It's like all the holidays combined! I promise you I will take great care of him and feed him extra treats for you. Or if you don't want your horse spoiled with treats, I will spend extra time hand grazing and grooming him. Actually, I do that regardless. Anyway, I will stop rambling now! Thank you again!*
>
> *—Tally"*

Tally emailed the note to Ryan with her question about how to address Pia and went back to her reading for history.

By the time she'd finished reading her two chapters, Tally had an email back from Ryan.

> *"Thanks, Tal, this is great. Fine to call her Pia. I sent it to her with your email address in case she wants to reply. See you tomorrow for your lesson on the magical Cam!"*

· CHAPTER 6 ·

Tally's second lesson on Cam was going so well she could barely stop smiling. She even got him to pick up his right lead after just a couple of tries. After a nice, long flat (Ryan loved to tell his riders, "you're only in the air for eight strides out of the whole course!") Tally, Maggie, and Mac all lined up in the center of the ring.

"Let's start with the plank off the left lead going toward the doors, around to your little gray oxer off the quarter line. Then up your outside line in five strides, and end on your diagonal single. Maggie, start us off," said Ryan.

Joey stepped right up into his canter from the walk and Maggie kept her seat light as she built her canter pace.

"Good, Mags, way to get your rhythm right away. That's a must in a smaller ring."

Maggie and Joey found the little green plank vertical with the flower boxes right out of stride. Tally thought back to jumping new flower boxes on Obie and how he'd stare at them as if he'd never seen flowers before.

Maggie guided Joey down the quarter line and made a soft right turn to the gray oxer, which featured a gray-and-white gate that Tally had helped paint a week prior.

"Be sure you stay over, Maggie, don't pop up too early. Now just sit chilly for the five strides, you've got plenty of step."

I wonder what Ryan will have me do to start, Tally thought as she watched Maggie and Joey jump the line and then the last single. *Probably just a single to start or something since we barely jumped the other day.*

"You're up, Tally, same thing," said Ryan.

Okay, then! Tally felt anxious to get started, but she wasn't nervous, exactly. Cam wasn't like the other horses and ponies she'd ridden before him. But Ryan also hadn't ever asked her to jump around like this without easing in first.

♘

"Good departure, now just keep that canter," he added. Tally counted her canter rhythm—*one, two, one, two*—as they approached the little plank jump.

"That's the way, Tally, now just ride forward and keep your eye up for the change. He's pretty automatic so you don't need to help him."

Tally felt Cam gather up behind to swap his lead from left to right after the plank. She also felt herself try to help him...before correcting herself and just riding straight. Tally shifted her hands right as they cantered down the quarter line to turn toward the gray oxer. Cam sailed over it easily, landing left. Tally felt his rhythm slow a little so she put more leg on as they approached the line.

"Good correction there when he slowed down a little. Eye up, think about the rhythm only," Ryan said. Coming out of the corner it was hard for Tally *not* to see her distance jumping in to the line. *Well that makes it easier*, she thought as they seamlessly found their jump in.

"Easy," Ryan said. "Your muscle memory wants you to put your leg on really strong in the lines from Obie but you don't need it here. Jump in, press for a stride, *then* see where you are and what you've got."

Cam built up a little on the way to the last single by the gate. Tally squeezed her fingers and sank down into her saddle—*one, two, one, two*—to steady him and they found a perfect medium distance. She cantered him through the corner before bringing him back down to the trot.

"Really good, Tal. You're doing a great job keeping your rhythm to the singles. We'll practice more lines in the next lesson to get you pressing for one stride and then relaxing. This horse isn't Obie or Goose. He knows his job," Ryan said, rubbing Cam's face as Tally brought him to a halt in front of her trainer. "Now you get to practice finessing your ride. Mac, hit it."

Mac took a deep breath before asking Sparkles to canter. They jumped the plank and the oxer well and cantered past the in-gate heading for the line.

"Easy here, you've built up a lot of pace," Ryan said. Sparkles gave a big exuberant jump in to the line and then Mac sat up and took back on the reins.

"Whoa," Tally heard Mac say as the pony compressed his stride, jumping out of the line nicely and keeping that canter down to the diagonal.

⊍

"*Good*, Mac!" said Ryan as she cantered away from the last jump. "Here's what I loved most about that ride: Even before I said it, you knew you'd built up more canter than you needed going to your outside five."

Mac nodded happily.

"That's great awareness and feel, and so you were able to adjust on the fly, and then keep what you needed to your last jump. Right on."

Everyone walked a couple of laps before heading back to the Field Ridge aisle. The high winds and thunderstorms were rolling back in that evening so the girls decided to hand-graze their horses since they wouldn't get turned out.

The air was warm for November as the ponies and Cam clip-clopped their way out of the barn and over to a grassy patch by the hill to the ring. Maggie and Mac chatted excitedly, on that high that you only get from a great lesson.

"I know Ryan will find someone who will love him, but I still wish *you* were leasing Joey," Mac said to Maggie.

"He's the best. I wish!" Maggie said, wrapping Joey's neck up in a hug. "My mom said no medium ponies."

U

"What does she have against medium ponies?" Mac asked, pretending to be horrified.

Maggie laughed. "It's not the ponies, it's me. I'd probably have a year at most on a medium—my sister is as tall as my mom already and she's only two years older than me. My pony career is going to be a short one."

Mac nodded and reached over to scratch Joey's back. Tally leaned against Cam's side while he grazed, as a cool breeze sent the trees into a gentle sway. She couldn't think of anywhere she'd rather be.

· CHAPTER 7 ·

"How was your lesson on Cam today?" Tally's dad asked as the family sat down to dinner.

"It was great. I kinda have to unlearn some of the stuff I was doing on Obie and Goose because this horse is such a packer."

"What does *a packer* mean?" asked her mom. She could be so cute, or sometimes annoying, depending on Tally's mood. Still on a high from her lesson, Tally found her mom's question endearing.

"It means the horse or the pony has had a lot of training and experience so they can just pack their rider around a course," Tally explained. "I haven't ridden one like this since...well, maybe ever?"

"What about the school horses?" asked her dad. "And Stacy, could you pass the mac and cheese?"

Tally's mom traded him the mac and cheese for a
bowl of peas, listening intently to the conversation.

"I wouldn't say school horses are packers. I mean
maybe one in, like, fifty could be a packer. But usually schoolies are...schoolies!" Tally said with a laugh.
"They are safe and patient and tolerate mistakes.
They have lots of different riders. There are different
challenges with a school horse. A lot of them want to
do things their way and they're more stubborn about
it than a horse who's not in a lesson program."

Tally's dad wiped his mouth and then put his nap-
kin back on his lap. "Tal, I am just so impressed with
all that you've learned over your time riding with Ryan.
You always loved it in the lesson program but now it's
like you've unlocked a whole new level of understanding
about the sport."

Tally rolled her eyes. "Dad—

"I mean it!" he said. "Do you know how many people
never have a passion like this? Plenty of kids play sports,
but do they come home and read about it and watch
videos, and go hang out at the field the way you hang
out in the barn? I love it, Tal. I'm really proud of you."

Tally smiled and her mom reached over to give her

hand a squeeze. "I am too, honey. It's amazing. As long as you stay safe and you prioritize school, I'm all for it. Speaking of safety, are you still in your vest every day?"

"Every ride, Mom."

"Good. Homework finished by bedtime, okay? And Ryan emailed us about a show coming up for you. He cc'd you, so check that out too," her mom added with a wink.

Tally cleaned up after dinner as fast as she could and then jogged up the stairs to read about the show. She flopped down on her bed with her laptop, opened the email and scanned it quickly...

"Low Children's Hunters...Cam can do 2'6" in his sleep...one-day show...November 13."

Wow, that's soon, she thought. Tally pictured the mini course she and Cam jumped in her lesson. She'd done harder things. She could show this horse.

Tally's email notification pinged. She had a new message from Pia.

Hi Tally,

It was great to hear from you and I am thrilled for you to enjoy Cam while I'm abroad. My wife and I were just talking about how my situation growing up with horses was much like yours, riding whatever horse was available. It would have been my dream to ride a horse like Cam back in those days, so it's my pleasure to give you that opportunity now. I really appreciate you taking that extra grooming and grazing time with him. I love doing the same. Treats are fine, I just like to save them for the end of a ride, rather than feeding them all the time. Cam is such a gentleman so I don't want to overdo it and risk him becoming pushy for his beloved apple nuggets! Have a great time with him. I can't wait to hear from Ryan about all your success in the show ring.

—Pia.

· CHAPTER 8 ·

"Let them walk a minute and then we'll jump around a bit."

Ryan walked across the large indoor ring to make some adjustments to the jumps. The new footing had been installed and the horses seemed happy. Tally even thought she could feel a difference, like the ground was lighter and more springy underneath them, though that might have been her imagination.

Maggie was going to try horses at a big sales barn a couple of hours away that afternoon, so Ryan was teaching lessons in the morning. It was just Tally and Mac in Ryan's lesson, but another instructor had her three students up in the big indoor, too. The vibe in the ring felt happy and excited, a lot like the schooling shows that Oaks hosted in this ring.

"Nicole's riders are going to stay out on the rail while you two jump a little course. They'll stay out of your way so just focus on your track," said Ryan. "Mac, you'll start us off. Left lead away from home to the green single. Then turn right and come up the diagonal line in seven strides. Down the judge's line in five, and end on the coop on the quarter line."

Mac nodded and Sparkles swished his tail as he stepped into his left lead canter. They kept a steady pace and Sparkles rounded over the green vertical, decorated with multiple flower boxes, and then landed on his right lead.

"Keep counting your rhythm," said Ryan. They jumped into the diagonal line, which reminded Tally of a horse show with its textured green rails. "Stop pulling, Mac. Leg. Leg!" Sparkles had to reach to get out over the second jump, another vertical with a white gate and green rails.

They came around to the outside and the pair looked picture-perfect as they met the vertical right out of stride.

"Now land and keep your leg on, don't take back," said Ryan. Sparkles got to the oxer just right this time.

‿

"Good! Keep this same rhythm to your coop," Ryan called. Sparkles skipped across the ground—he had that same gorgeous, straight-legged canter as Joey, Tally thought—ears perked forward as they arrived at the shiny coop.

"Really good ride, Mac Attack," Ryan said, gesturing for her to come toward the middle of the ring. "I think your muscle memory is the reason you're slowing down a little in the lines. Joey needed that when he got forward, right?"

Mac nodded. "But this isn't Joey," she said.

"Exactly," Ryan replied, clapping his hands lightly together. "This pony is more sensitive. Joey went in a corkscrew bit, while this pony goes in just a plain snaffle. That's a clue for you about how differently they go. Sparkles is more sensitive, so if you make a mistake and whoa in your lines, he's going to listen to you, compress his stride, and you're going to meet that out with a long, gappy distance. You don't need to *add* leg in the lines, you just need to keep your leg on and stay the same. Make sense?"

Mac nodded happily and stroked her pony's neck.

"Tally, same thing."

As Tally and Cam approached the first jump, she noticed the students from the other lesson walking in toward the middle of the ring. In addition to Ryan and Mac, the other three students and their instructor were all watching her, too.

Count your rhythm. One, two, one, two.

A perfect medium distance showed up to the green vertical. Tally focused on staying straight and then turning her head for the lead change. As Ryan had told her, Cam was pretty auto in his changes, but if Tally didn't indicate where they were turning, the change could get sticky. And the indoor ring was so big that it wasn't always obvious to the horse which way they'd turn after each jump.

"That's enough canter right there, Tal," said Ryan. "Land into the line and press for a stride and then see where you are." Tally kept her hip angle closed and put her leg on as they landed from the vertical. She could feel Cam push from behind, his front end becoming lighter, as she counted seven strides to the out. She glanced down to see Cam already on his left lead.

"Don't look for your lead, Tally, you ride better

than that. I know you can feel it," Ryan called as they rounded the short side. Tally shifted her hands left to turn for the five-stride line. After the jump in, she pressed with her lower legs for a stride.

"Good, now *easy*," Ryan told her. The jump out of the line came up fast, but Cam was such a pro that their jump felt just as good as an ideal, more medium distance.

One, two, one, two, Tally counted, still acutely aware of how many people were watching her. It was so quiet in the ring as they approached the coop.

One, two, one, two, one. Tally reminded herself to stay over on the back side, and she heard a light swoosh of Cam's tail as they cantered away from their last jump.

"Very good, Tal, give him a pat. Did you feel how when you pressed for a stride in the seven, your jump out came up just right, but when you pressed in the five, you rushed him out a little?" Tally nodded. "Why do you think that is?"

"I did a bigger press in the five," Tally told him, halting in the middle next to Mac.

"Yup. Just got a little overzealous there. One

medium press, assess where you are in the line, and then adjust your stride length as needed, right? Both of you rode really well today, nice job. You can walk the ponies out in the outdoor if you'd like."

CHAPTER 9

"Tally, that was so good!" Mac squealed as the girls walked through the in-gate of the outdoor ring. Mac let the reins slide through her fingers as Sparkles stretched his neck out. Tally let Cam do the same as she fell in step next to her friend.

"Thanks. He's perfect, like everyone says."

"You look great on him," Mac added. "Really, it's been like a week and you're already nailing courses."

"Um, so are you!" said Tally.

Mac smiled broadly. "Mr. Sparklepants, you are awesome," she said, bending down to rub both sides of her new pony's neck. "My parents said they want to buy him, and Ryan already has someone lined up to lease Joey. It should be finalized really soon. I can't believe he's leaving the barn."

"I know," Tally said, wrinkling her nose. "But you'd be a lot sadder if it weren't for this guy."

Mac nodded. "True. Hey, do you think you'll do the show next weekend?"

"Yup. I can't believe I'm showing after such a short time. But Cam is used to the three-foot, so this should be super easy for him. So, what will you show Sparkles in? The larges?"

"Yes! I thought maybe Ryan would want me to start in the children's ponies since Sparkles and I are so new to each other, but he said I'm riding really well...plus, the large ponies jump two-nine, which is only one hole higher than the mediums, who jump two-six, so we're going for it." Mac was beaming atop her new pony. Tally remembered how Mac worried about her progress with Joey when the girls first got to know each other. Mac had been so proud to put in good rounds at the big shows in the Medium Pony Hunters, or "the division," as it was called for all three sizes of pony hunters—small, medium or large.

It was actually Mac who taught her about "the division," and about showing ponies in general. Coming from the lesson program at the Oaks riding school,

Tally hadn't known the details at the time: Small ponies, who stood 12.2 hands or smaller, jumped 2'3" in the Small Pony Hunters. Medium ponies, 12.3 hands to 13.2 hands, jumped 2'6," and large ponies, 13.3 hands to 14.2 hands, jumped 2'9."

Tally nodded toward the gate. "Want to take them down the walking path back to the barn?"

"Let's go," said Mac.

Once Sparkles and Cam had been untacked and brushed, Brenna walked over from the school aisle to Field Ridge.

"Hey girls, we are going to keep night turnout going just a little bit longer while it stays warm like this. You can put them both in their medium turnout blankets. Oh, and Tally, instead of the evening shift tomorrow, would you be able to start right after school?"

Tally nodded. "I'll double check with my mom but I'm sure it will be fine."

"Thanks," said Brenna. "How are the new partnerships going?"

Mac and Tally looked at each other, breaking into huge, silly grins.

U

"They're amazing," said Mac. "So good. And it's only been a week, which is bizarre."

"Not when you find a great match!" Brenna said. "You too, Tally? I mean, half the barn wishes they could ride this horse."

"I feel really lucky," Tally answered honestly. "He is so much fun to ride and *so* sweet."

Brenna smiled and turned to walk back toward the school aisle. "Keep up the great work, girls!"

Tally followed Mac into the tack room where Mac propped her foot up on her trunk and pulled a stick of boot polish out from a small grooming tote.

"I do it after riding now because I never remember, or leave enough time, *before* I ride," Mac explained with a laugh.

Tally smiled, her eyes wandering to the oversized Field Ridge white board behind her friend. On one side of the board, Ryan wrote out each day's lessons, hacks, and training rides. The other side was either left blank, featured a scheduling reminder for the barn, or a quote that Ryan wanted to share with everyone. Today was a quote day.

"If you are not rooting for everyone at the horse

show, you are on the wrong team."

"Did you read that?" Tally asked.

Mac looked over at the board, pausing in silence as she took it in. "That," she said, "is awesome."

· CHAPTER 10 ·

The next day at school, the seventh and eighth graders had an optional assembly about the upcoming winter sports and theater season. Those who didn't want to attend could go to a longer lunch instead, which was just where Tally was headed when she saw Jacob ahead of her by a locker.

"Hey, Jacob!" she shouted. Jacob glanced over his shoulder and gave her the smallest of nods. Tally jogged to catch up.

"Hey, are you going to lunch? Wait, what's wrong?" Jacob looked like he'd been crying.

"I don't know. I guess I should go to the assembly and find a new sport."

"A new sport?" Tally asked. "Why?"

"Carlo is never going to be sound enough to show

again," said Jacob, his voice barely above a whisper.

Tally exhaled audibly. "Well, playing lacrosse isn't going to make that any better. Come on, let's get lunch and we can talk?"

They picked up the Monday cafeteria staples—a turkey sandwich, fruit cup, and chocolate milk—and found a table by the window.

"So, what happened," Tally asked, poking her straw into the milk carton.

Jacob dropped his backpack at his feet and kept his eyes down at his lap. "The injury was a strain in Carlo's suspensory ligament, so everyone was hopeful he could recover. My mom was hopeful, Ryan was hopeful, the rehab barn was hopeful. They started to bring him back into work to see if he would stay sound. He's mostly okay but they call it, um, 'serviceably sound.' So...yeah. He can flat and he can probably do poles and cavaletti a couple times a week, but he'll never go back to the show ring."

"That's so sad. I'm really sorry," Tally said.

Jacob shrugged. "I'm super sad but, like, I'm happy too because we came up with a good plan for him. Ryan said a lot of times with a suspensory, that's it. The horse lives the rest of their lives out in a field. Actually, I'm not sure Carlo would be sad about that." Jacob flashed the smallest of smiles. "But I mean, eventually, he'd get bored. So, I'm happy with the solution. We are going to donate him to a school that probably can use him in lessons or on an IEA team or an IHSA team."

Tally and Jacob were both quiet for a moment before Jacob spoke again.

"Ryan said that when you donate a horse to a school like we're going to do with Carlo, they get to have a life afterward. It's like a new career for him, even though it's not the same as showing. I'll really miss him." Jacob looked down again, kicking at his backpack with his foot.

"Maybe he'll be really happy doing the IEA or IHSA shows," Tally offered. "They have lots of flat classes, right? So, he'll show again, he just won't jump?"

"Yeah, he does love the excitement of a horse show," said Jacob, perking up a little. "I think he'll be okay. It's just that he's the only horse I've ever had, and my mom isn't ready to talk about getting another one. She did say I could keep taking lessons at Quince Oaks though. Twice a week once the rehab is paid off."

"Well that's good news," Tally said. "I rode in the lesson program for like, five years before Ryan even came to the barn."

"You did?"

"Yeah. I actually didn't know anything about A-rated shows, or about showing outside of Oaks schooling shows. I've gone back to the lesson program too, in between projects for Ryan. I still get a little jealous sometimes when you ride Sweetie," she added with a laugh.

"She's a good horse," Jacob said, looking a bit happier now as he tore off the plastic seal from his fruit cup. "I rode Scout a couple of times, too, he's a lot of fun. Two lessons a week will be good, it's just not the same as having a horse that's mine, you know?"

Tally nodded. "I've never technically had my own horse, but with the catch rides, they've been mine for weeks or even months at a time. But it's really hard when they get sold. Or go back to their owners."

The friends sat in silence for a minute as they dug into their lunches. Tally glanced around the cafeteria, only about a quarter full.

"You really wanted to join everybody in that theater

and sports assembly?" she asked Jacob.

He laughed. "No, I was just feeling sorry for myself. You're right, it's not that big a deal to Carlo once he's settled in a new place. He'll like his new job. And I bet I can get my mom to let me do the whole Oaks series. Have you seen those long ribbons they give out for year-end? I heard there are going to be bigger prizes this year, too."

Tally thought of her own third place ribbon, hanging in her room from the series she did with Sweetie. She thought about Carlo, too. Even though donating him was sad for Jacob, he and his mom were doing the right thing by their horse.

· CHAPTER 11 ·

Tally was watering the horses on the school aisle to wrap up her working student shift on Wednesday afternoon when Maggie bounded up to her, catching her by surprise.

"Hey!" Maggie said, more excited than Tally had ever seen her.

"Wow, you scared me," Tally said with a start, the water from the bucket sloshing out onto her shoes. "If I get frostbite it's going to be all your fault," she added, shaking off her sneaker.

"I'm sorry! I'm just so excited. My new horse comes today! *My* horse, can you believe it?"

"Wow, that was fast! Congrats!" said Tally, dragging the hose to the end of the aisle. Maggie followed her, bouncing on the balls of her feet.

"We tried three at this big sales barn and the horses were all awesome but super different from each other. One was really forward and had horse show miles in the jumpers and equitation, so Ryan said we should pass on it since I want to do the hunters. The next was super fancy but too green. And the third reminds me of Obie a little bit. Kind of a push ride but super sweet, really comfortable, and he's got this round, lofty jump. That's the one we got."

Tally arrived at the hose station and pushed the water spout down to turn off the flow. "I've never tried horses before, that sounds really fun," she said.

"It was awesome. We agreed to do a six-month lease with the option to buy," said Maggie.

"What's that?" asked Tally.

"I hadn't heard of it either, but it's like, you lease the horse for six months no matter what, and at the end of it, you can apply the lease fee to the purchase price if you buy the horse. Or if it doesn't work out, you give the horse back and look for another," said Maggie.

Tally felt a little wave of jealousy. *No, YOU look for another*, she thought. *Not me.* Then she thought of Cam waiting for her in his stall, and all the fun they still had ahead of them. She really was lucky to have him, and all the others Ryan had given her to ride. She'd figure out a way to buy her own horse someday.

"So, what's his name? And when do you get to ride him?" she asked Maggie.

"Field Day. Isn't that a fun show name? His barn name is Pete. Ryan is riding him this afternoon, so I'm going to go watch. I'll have my first lesson on him tomorrow." Maggie was practically jogging down the boarder aisle. "How's it going with Cam?"

"Great," Tally said as the girls arrived at the Field Ridge tack room. "We are showing this weekend, which seems really soon but I'm excited."

"You'll be awesome," said Maggie. "Okay, I'm going to head up to the big indoor so I don't miss any of Ryan's ride. See you up there?"

"See ya!" said Tally. She gathered up her saddle, pads, and bridle and walked it all over to Cam's stall.

"Hi, sweet boy," she greeted him. Cam flicked an ear at her from a large pile of hay in the corner of his stall. Tally took her time getting him groomed and tacked. When he lifted his head to greet her, she noticed how he held still while she rubbed his face.

She even put her cheek on his and just stood there for a moment. It was so cool to feel bonded with a horse in such a short time.

Up at the ring, Ryan trotted by on a small gray horse. Tally noticed Ryan's spurs were low on his boots. He once told her he did that to avoid inadvertently using the spur—it was easier to use a spur by mistake when they sat higher on your boots.

"Once you get him into gear it's not so much work to get him to carry you," Ryan was telling Maggie, who watched from the in-gate. "I'm using my spurs one at a time through the turns to get him engaged. A horse like this can't just go around and around in circles. If he's bored, he'll be that much harder to get moving. Hey, Tally."

Tally gave Ryan a little wave and walked Cam over to the mounting block. Ryan had worked with all of his students over the summer to get every horse standing patiently while their riders mounted, to avoid another accident like Mac's. Once Tally had both of her stirrups, she squeezed Cam forward to walk on the rail. After one lap, she changed direction and worked on some leg yields before asking the horse to do more.

The temperature had dropped again and Tally wanted to make sure Cam was thoroughly warmed up.

At the other end of the ring, Ryan was cantering a large circle on Pete. Maggie's new horse was little, but Tally could tell he had a big stride. Ryan came off the circle and popped over a small vertical on the quarter line. The horse looked like fun—Tally was happy for Maggie.

"You ready to do some work, buddy?" Tally asked Cam, who appeared to nod in agreement.

She squeezed him with both calves and he stepped up into his trot with a swish of his tail. Tally smiled. Even the way Cam picked up a trot felt fancy.

As Tally put her leg on to ask for more trot, Cam tossed his head. She felt him hop up a little behind, too.

"That's what he does when he's fresh," Ryan called to her. "Keep putting your leg on and he'll knock it off soon. It's just because it's cold."

Tally squeezed, and Cam tossed his head. Squeeze. Head toss. It was like the horse was drawing circles in the air with his nose.

"I know, buddy, you'll feel better when you're warm," she whispered, moving Cam off the rail and onto a serpentine.

It didn't take long for Cam to settle in. He stretched out his neck, his body more relaxed, as Tally moved into trotting circles after their serpentine. When it was time to canter, the ring had cleared out. Tally asked Cam to extend his canter down the long sides and collect on the short sides. Brenna's dog, an affectionate terrier mix named Spud, lay down by the ingate, lazily keeping an eye on Tally and Cam as they worked.

· CHAPTER 12 ·

That Friday, Tally went straight to the barn from school for her last lesson before the horse show. By the time they started jumping, she was pretty sure it was the best lesson she'd had in a long time.

"That's it, Tally, great! You're figuring him out now," said Ryan as they jumped into a line. "Just keep that canter to your oxer."

Tally felt a click with Cam that she was pretty sure only happened when a horse was as good, and as special, as this one. The adjustment period had been so much shorter with him than with her other rides. Maybe that was part of what made him a packer.

Turning left and lining up the final oxer of their course, Tally felt the urge to cut her turn, something she did when she was anxious or excited to get to a jump. She reminded herself to count her rhythm.

"You got a little excited there, didn't you?" Ryan asked. *Mind reader.* "He's a lot of fun, I know, but don't rush your jump. Let the oxer come to you."

One, two, one, two, one, Tally counted, letting her body relax as Cam took off. Her old instructor Meg used to say that the movement of the horse's jump should open the rider's knee angle and close their hip angle. It was funny how a random memory like that could pop into her head in the split second she spent in the air over a jump.

"That's the ride!" said Ryan. "I don't think Cam needs to do any more. You don't either, that was great, Tally. Let him walk a couple laps on the buckle."

Tally let her reins go long and rubbed Cam's neck. He let out a little snort and poked his nose out, stretching as far as he could go.

"Okay, Mags, you're up, let's try again. Just the outside line to your oxer."

Tally's stomach dropped a little for her friend. Maggie's excitement over Pete the other day had been replaced with frustration in their lesson together.

Maggie went to pick up the left lead canter but Pete stepped into his right lead instead.

"That happened because you're leaning!" said Ryan. "Again, this isn't Joey. This horse will tell on you each time you ask for something with your body. You need to ask with your leg. Now sit straight, keep your eyes up, and outside leg hard."

Pete picked up his left lead and Maggie looked relieved. They turned toward the line and Pete drifted to the left before Maggie steered him back to the right.

"Too much hand!" called Ryan. "Circle and try that turn again. Use mostly your legs to turn and just *shift* your hands left. He knows what to do, so you need to be softer in how you tell him."

Tally could practically feel Maggie's frustration as she came around to the line again. This time they were straighter, but Pete had to add in an extra, choppy stride at the base of the vertical before jumping it.

"That's okay, you're just used to the pony stride and have to adjust to a horse stride," said Ryan. Pete had landed without much impulsion so he and Maggie added a stride up the line.

"Count your rhythm to your single. There was one less stride to the in of the line, right?" Ryan asked. Maggie nodded and turned to the oxer.

"That was better, using your legs and just shifting your hands there," said Ryan. "One, two, one, two, just hold that rhythm and keep your eye up. Leave his mouth alone and you won't add that extra stride."

Maggie and Pete found a nice distance to the oxer and Maggie looked happy to be on the other side.

"There you go! A learning curve is normal, Mags, this is all good stuff. You're going to learn a lot from this horse."

Tally recognized the expression on Maggie's face. Her friend looked like she was doing everything she could not to cry.

Down at the barn, Mac was coming in for her lesson as Tally was packing her bag to go home.

"Nice of you to ride with us today," Tally said, playfully rolling her eyes.

"My mom won't let me quit piano," said Mac. "So, I have to do a later lesson on Fridays now. How was Cam?"

"He's perfect," Tally said, beaming. "I'm so excited to show tomorrow."

"Me too! Did Maggie ride her new horse today? I just walked past Pete's stall but I didn't see her anywhere."

"Yeah, her mom just picked her up. I think Pete is

harder than she expected. They had kind of a tough lesson."

Mac wrinkled her nose and set her bag down in front of Sparkles' stall. "That sucks. It's not easy in the beginning when you're getting to know them. Especially if they're not the ride you're used to. Oh, did I tell you Joey left for his new lease this morning?"

"No!" said Tally, glancing down the aisle toward Joey's old stall. "Are you okay?"

"Yeah," Mac said with a nod. Sparkles stuck his head out over the stall guard and Mac stroked his neck. "The girl who's leasing him is super nice and she said I can come visit and bring him carrots anytime. That helps a lot. I think I'd be a lot sadder about it if he were being leased across the country or something, you know?"

Tally nodded.

"I'll see you at the show tomorrow?" Mac asked.

Tally watched her mom pull up outside the aisle. "Can't wait, see you then!"

U

· CHAPTER 13 ·

Tally woke up with a huge knot in her stomach.

Cam is perfect. Cam is a packer. And then the thought she kept trying to ignore: *I have to be perfect, too.*

She took her time getting dressed, making sure that every last detail was perfect. Ryan noticed everything, down to socks that peek out from show boots, or hair nets visible below a helmet line.

"Tally! Five minutes! What can I bring you in the car for breakfast?" called her mom.

"A bagel, thanks!" Tally called back. From the hook in her closet, she grabbed her favorite belt—black leather with a blue stripe—and fastened it neatly over the button on her breeches. Then she turned around in front of her full-length mirror to make sure her show shirt was tucked in evenly all the way around.

Finally, she zipped and buttoned up her show coat. Her division was the first of the day, so she may as well arrive at the show all ready to go.

Tally jogged down the stairs and took her warmest puffer vest out of the hall closet. It was only a little above freezing outside. Ryan often reminded them that riders, just like their horses, needed to stay warm and loose before competing.

Twenty minutes later, Tally stood at the in-gate with Ryan, who was talking her through her first course. Tally was happily surprised to find that once he told her the first jump, she was able to guess the rest. Hunter courses at shows typically started with a single vertical and then made a figure-eight type pattern from there.

"How do you feel?" Ryan asked her.

"Good. Ready to go," Tally said.

"Great. And Tal? I expect you to make mistakes in the show ring. I hope you know that. You need to make mistakes, and you need to make them in the show ring, because that's how you learn. We're here to have fun. Cam is a blast. Just enjoy it."

Tally smiled and nodded, wondering how Ryan so often seemed to know just what she was thinking. She took a deep breath. He was right—no one was perfect, so it was a losing battle trying to ride a perfect course.

Ryan talked her through the second course as well, adding that the third course was the same as the first. This was a one-day A show, so the division went all at once, rather than split between two days.

"Look who's here," said Lupe, the Field Ridge head groom, walking up to Tally with Cam. The horse looked handsome as ever tacked up and ready to show. Tally felt a flicker of disappointment that he wasn't braided—on the rare occasion that she did get to show a braided horse, it felt like a big deal. Field Ridge often competed at this particular facility, set on the campus of a private school with a big equestrian program. Ryan seemed to know when it was customary to braid and when they could skip it.

"We're still looking for a first group of riders to start us off in the combined Low Children's and Low Adult Hunters," the announcer said on the PA.

"Want to go first?" Ryan asked. "I'll put you in for that first group if you do."

"Sure," Tally said eagerly. She couldn't wait to hear her name and Cameron's announced in the ring. It felt like a dream come true just to be here with him.

Lupe lead Cam to the mounting block and Tally climbed aboard.

"Come on out here to the warm-up ring, Tal," Ryan said, gesturing to the outdoor ring. "The footing is good, not frozen yet. Oh, hey, Lupe, are you good for the December plan?"

Lupe nodded his head yes. "You got it."

"Great," said Ryan. "Tally, trot a couple laps in either direction and then we'll jump one or two and you'll be set."

Tally walked Cam out to the rail, reminding herself that unlike her previous mounts, she didn't have to brace herself for a spook or any green behavior for this one. Cam had been doing this for far longer than she had. It was kind of cool that she had such an experienced horse to show her the way.

After a couple laps at the trot and canter, Ryan asked her to walk while he set a plain white vertical in the middle of the ring. Another trainer had come in to claim the other one.

"Tally, catch your left lead and come get this vertical here. Remember, he likes to drift right, so put your right leg on before, during, and after your left turn."

Tally did as she was instructed, squeezing Cam's right side and then giving him a light thump with it when he still wanted to bulge.

"Good correction there, now keep flowing out of the turn," said Ryan.

Tally had heard of riders seeing their distance from as far away as the corner. And while she didn't know exactly how many strides she had to go, when she turned toward a jump on Cam, she felt totally confident that they would find a medium distance as long as she kept his rhythm and straightness. Cam was magical that way.

"Great!" said Ryan. "Now come off the right lead."

Tally slowed Cam to a walk, insinuated a right turn to pick up that lead, and kept his forward canter through the turn to the jump the next time.

"You're good, keep flowing," said Ryan. They met the vertical just right and Ryan said they were done.

Tally's butterflies returned, but she was excited to get into the show ring. Back at the in-gate, Ryan asked her to recite the course one more time and then patted Cam on the shoulder.

⚘

"Remember, right leg through the left turns and keep your rhythm. Have fun," he said.

Tally walked through the gate and took a deep breath in and out. Their plan was to show off Cam's nice, big trot down the long side and then pick up the right lead in the corner, where it would be easier on his tricky direction.

"First hunter trip is in the ring, this is number 219, Cameron, ridden by Tally Hart," said the announcer. Tally smiled when she heard their names.

This was it. Time to have fun.

CHAPTER 14

Tally came out of her first right turn to a single birch vertical feeling just as confident as she had in the schooling ring. She didn't see her distance exactly, but she could feel that she was on the right pace for it to show up.

One, two, one, two, she counted, keeping up her usual habit to maintain Cam's rhythm. *One, two, one,* she whispered, softly closing her hip angle as he left the ground. Cam felt exactly the same in the show ring as he did at home.

She rode him straight toward the corner, confident without looking down that he'd landed on his preferred left lead. Tally made sure to keep riding straight and shift her hands right through the turn. The next jump was an oxer on the long side of the ring. The standards were shaped and painted like pine trees and the rails were wrapped in the fuzzy green material Tally recognized from other shows. She felt Cam step up out of the corner as they approached the oxer.

One, two, one, two, she counted as Cam cantered to the jump, finding another great distance. The rest of the course unfolded ahead of her like a dream. The diagonal six-stride line was next and Ryan told her she would likely need to move up, even though it was heading toward the gate when horses naturally added pace. Tally kept a steady leg, adding pressure for the final three strides, and Cam worked out the rest, opening up his canter just enough to meet the oxer well for the out. Then they went up the judge's line in five strides, and home across a bending line in six.

"Aim for the middle of both jumps in the bending line and it should come right up," Ryan had told her as they'd studied the track together before Tally got on.

Coming out of her final turn, Tally noticed she needed even more leg to keep Cam's impulsion. "Good boy," she whispered, "just one more line."

She jumped in straight to the line, looking for the jump out while still in the air over the first jump.

Land, one, two, she counted, before remembering that Ryan told her to always land and squeeze for at least the first stride, since Cam wasn't the most naturally forward ride.

Whoops. Guess I'll have to do that now! Tally thought to herself.

Squeeze, three, squeeze, four...okay we're there... five, six.

Cam's jump felt round and nearly effortless over the final oxer, which was built up to look solid with its flower boxes and gate. Cam landed his right lead—*did the horse know this was the last jump of the line?*—and Ryan whooped at the gate. Lupe joined him, as did some other people who likely recognized Cam from the show circuit. Tally practically felt like a celebrity getting to ride this horse, and gave him an appreciative pat during their closing circle.

The second trip went a lot like the first, and on the third trip, Tally found a somewhat tight distance into the final line off a left turn. She had to really move up to get out of the line in the six strides.

"Do you know why that happened?" Ryan asked when they came out of the ring.

"It's all kind of a blur, sorry," Tally said, her breath coming out in cold puffs.

"Don't apologize, this is how you learn. You lost your distance there because you let him drift. If you'd added more right leg to keep him straight, the in of that line would have come right up," said Ryan. "Does that make sense?"

"Yes," Tally said with a nod. "But I thought I did have my right leg on through each of the left turns?"

"You probably did, but the more tired Cam gets— that was your third trip, remember—the more he's going to want to drift. All horses kind of revert to these types of habits as they get tired. By the third trip, you're going to need even more right leg. It's a good reminder to ride what you have, what's underneath you, in every course. It takes time to learn how to really be in the moment at each jump when you've got the horse show nerves, too."

"So more right leg would have kept him straighter and we wouldn't have chipped in," said Tally, closing her eyes as she visualized it.

"Exactly. You're doing great, Tal, this is the fine-tuning stuff that we'll improve over time. You've got some time to relax now, and loosen Cam's girth. It'll be a while before you hack."

Tally dismounted and gave Cam a big squeeze around his neck. "Thanks, buddy," she whispered. "Lupe, would you hold him for a minute so I can grab a water?"

"Sure thing, super star," Lupe answered with a wink.

CHAPTER 15

"...Number 219..."

Tally glanced around nervously. She'd entered the ring for the under-saddle class and had been looking around at the jumps on the long sides of the ring. The jump crew had removed the rails, gates, and boxes so that riders could utilize the lines in the hack class. Was she in the wrong place? She focused her attention back on the announcer.

"Second place is number 464, Linguini, ridden by Charlie Hunter."

Oh my gosh, we won? Tally felt her face flush. She'd heard her number announced but was so focused on the ring that she'd missed the context.

"We won, Cam!" she whispered, rubbing Cam's neck.

"In the second over fences, your winner again is 219, Cameron, and Tally Hart."

Tally beamed as she brought Cam back down to a walk and took a peek at the judges' box. The judge was walking to the middle of the ring to watch the class, something Tally hadn't seen before.

The announcer rattled off numbers in the third over fences class, calling Tally and Cam's names sixth. *Wow, a small mistake and we're in the middle of the pack. It must be good competition today.*

"Riders, this is your class. You're now being judged at the walk…And, go ahead and trot please, riders, all trot."

Out of the corner of her eye, Tally saw a gray horse and rider coming in between her and the judge.

"Turn early so you can get seen on the other side, Tal," she heard Ryan say from the in-gate. Tally checked the traffic and then turned left across the middle of the ring in order to pass in front of the judge on the far quarter line. When they came around the next time, Tally checked out where the other horses were earlier in order to catch the judge's eye again.

As the flat class went on, Tally felt like she got

better and better at making sure Cam got time in front of the judge. He was a good mover, so she knew how important it was to show him off. Particularly his big, lofty trot.

Tally brought Cam in the lineup and she could make out the results over the radio before the announcer called them out. Cam was fourth! When the announcer made it official, she gave Cam a big pat and caught a glimpse of Ryan clapping at the in-gate.

"And we've also got your tricolors in the Low Children's, Low Adult Hunters. Champion with twenty-two and a half points is Cameron, with Tally Hart in the irons."

Ryan whooped. Tally blushed. Mac beamed at her from the ground.

"You were champion! Have you been champion at a rated show before?" Mac asked.

"A couple times with Goose," Tally said, grinning.

"Well, still, this is big," Mac insisted. "First championship in the Low Children's!"

"Go take a hundred pictures, girls. And send me the best one to share on social media, okay?" Ryan attached the blue, red, and yellow ribbon to Cam's bridle.

♘

The horse lifted his head a little higher as they walked out of the ring to take photos.

Later that morning, while Cam happily munched on hay from his hay net in the trailer, Tally stood at the in-gate to watch Mac's first time in the show ring with Sparklepants. She loved staying in her show outfit while spectating, her clothes telling everyone she'd competed there, too.

"That pace is just right, keep it there, Mac," Ryan said as Mac cantered by the in-gate. Tally counted the pace in her head as she watched the new pony skip across the ring. He "walked the lines," as Tally had heard people say, meeting the oxers just right, or even a little bit tight, but jumping out beautifully each time.

Tally clapped for her friend after each of her trips and felt nearly overwhelmed with happiness when she saw Mac's smile leaving the ring.

"Each trip got a little better, didn't it, Mac?" Ryan asked. Mac nodded eagerly.

"And you started out with a super solid trip! Improving on that each time is impressive. You're in the groove, and I'm really proud of you." Ryan gave Sparkle a stroke on his shoulder. "Grab a drink if you need one—there's a lot in this division so you both get a little break before you hack."

Mac dismounted and rubbed her new pony in front of his saddle.

"You guys were awesome!" said Tally. "You look like you've been riding him for years."

"Thanks, Tal. I can't believe it wasn't harder. It took me so many shows to be able to do this on Joey. I think he'd be proud of me," Mac said, giggling.

"He would. I'm sure of it. Want to go get a hot chocolate?"

"Yes!" Mac linked her arm into Tally's and they turned for the food stand.

U

· CHAPTER 16 ·

Tally didn't get back to the barn until Tuesday after the horse show. She'd diligently labeled and hung her ribbons in her room and felt like she'd been counting down the hours until she made it back to Cam. He had Sunday and Monday off of work, and Ryan told her to flat Tuesday and then they would lesson on Wednesday.

The door to the tack room was closed when Tally's mom dropped her off at the Field Ridge aisle. *That's odd...*

"Cam! I missed you!" Tally let herself into the horse's stall as Cam lifted his head to greet her.

"You've got hay in your mane," she said with a laugh, picking a piece out of Cam's forelock just as the tack room door opened.

"I'll see you up there, okay?" she heard Ryan telling someone.

"Hey, Tal," he greeted her as he passed Cam's stall.

"Hi," she replied, wondering what the closed-door meeting could have been about.

Tally had Cam nearly ready when she heard something a few stalls over. She twisted Cam's reins and looped his throatlatch through them in order to safely leave him in his stall with his bridle on—a school horse trick she'd learned from riding in the lesson program.

"Be right back, buddy," she whispered, and headed in the direction of the sound. Maggie had her back to Tally inside Pete's stall.

"Hey. You okay?"

Maggie sniffed and turned toward Tally but kept her eyes on the stall floor. "Not really."

"What's wrong?" Tally asked.

"I just met with Ryan about my show goals, and what we'll do with Pete over these next six months to see if he's a good fit. I was so excited to show in the Low Children's, but Ryan says he wants us to start in a two-foot division."

Maggie took a shaky breath before continuing.

"It's so embarrassing. I was showing in the two-six on Joey, and even before that on school horses. Now I have to take this giant step down because..." Maggie's voice trailed off.

"Because why?" Tally asked gently.

"Because I can't ride Pete." The gray horse turned to face Maggie at the mention of his name. Still looking down, she stroked his thick forelock.

"You *can* ride Pete. You are riding him," Tally said. "You just have to take the time to figure him out and get to know each other better."

"But what about you and Mac? You guys adjusted to your new horses like it was nothing. I chip in to like, every line."

"Maybe we adjusted fast on these horses, but it's not always like this. Remember what it was like for me with Obie? I couldn't get him to canter more than one long side of the ring."

Maggie sniffled—and smiled.

"I'm serious!" Tally continued. "Mac used to have trouble finding distances on Joey, too. It happens to everyone."

Both girls were quiet for a moment.

"Oh, and I fell off at the first jump in my first show with Ryan."

"*You* did? But you're...so good," said Maggie.

"Thanks," Tally answered with a smile. "So are you."

Maggie looked up and smiled back at her.

"I'm going to go up to the ring to flat Cam. You okay?" Tally asked. "I'll see you up there?"

"I'm okay. Thanks, Tally."

As Tally was wrapping up a long and loose flat session for Cam, Maggie was beginning her private lesson with Ryan. Tally took an extra couple of laps walking Cam on the buckle in order to see how Maggie was doing.

"Think about asking for your left lead now, before you actually ask," Ryan said as Tally halted Cam in the middle of the ring to dismount. "Think about sitting straight and keeping your eyes up before you ask."

Maggie tilted her chin up as she and Pete approached the far corner of the ring at the trot. Tally noticed what a cute mover he was at the trot.

"Good Maggie, now just be mindful about where your body is when you ask. Stay centered over both stirrups."

Tally watched as Maggie tilted her chin up once more and closed her hip angle as Pete stepped into the left lead canter.

"That's it! Good, Mags!" said a triumphant Ryan. "See? You're figuring him out already. One transition at a time."

· CHAPTER 17 ·

At school that Thursday, Tally sat down next to Jacob in the cafeteria.

"Hey," he said. "I was just going to look for you. I have so much to tell you."

Tally opened her lunchbox and pulled out an apple; then quickly tucked it into her backpack. Cam would enjoy it even more than she would. "Tell me!"

"Well, my mom and I visited the school that hosts the IEA team and it was awesome. They have huge turnouts and the barn is really nice. We decided to donate Carlo there."

"That's great!" Tally said, pulling apart sides of a string cheese wrapper.

Jacob smiled. "And my mom said I could half-lease Scout since I won't have a horse of my own for a while probably. Brenna told me we might even be able to go to shows off the property with him."

"That's so cool," Tally said. "I didn't know they were half-leasing school horses! Wait, no Sweetie?"

"Sweetie is my favorite, but Ryan thinks I'm getting too tall for her."

Tally nodded. "How tall is Scout?"

"He's got to be sixteen hands, maybe sixteen-one or -two. I can't wait to get started. It's two lessons a week and one day to flat alone with the half lease."

"That's perfect," Tally said, just as their friend Ava sat down at the table with them.

"Hey, nice 'leo,'" said Jacob with an approving nod.

"Too much to wear to school?" asked Ava, doing a shimmy so that the sparkles on her leotard caught the light from beneath her hoodie.

"Never," said Tally with a grin. "How's gymnastics going?"

"Good. Hard. Look at this," Ava said, opening her hands to show Tally and Jacob her right palm.

"Um, that is a *hole*," said Jacob, his eyes wide.

"Yup. I'm doing giants on the bars now—that's when you swing your body all the way around, 360

◡

degrees—and it really tears up your hands."

"That's worse than getting rubs from your stirrup leathers!" said Tally.

Ava settled into her seat and unzipped her lunch box. "So, how are the ponies?"

"Good," said Tally. "I'm showing in the Low Children's on this lady's Adult Amateur horse and he's the most fun ever. And Jacob is going to half-lease Scout from the riding school."

Jacob nodded and smiled, while Ava put down her sandwich and looked at Tally thoughtfully.

"You're getting like, a lot of catch rides," she said.

"I guess," said Tally with a shrug.

"That's such a big compliment. You could be a professional one day."

Tally paused and thought about the idea of working with horses every day. She'd always assumed she'd go into something having to do with science, maybe even vet school.

"No, seriously, you could be a professional and show all year long. You could ride and compete yourself, *and* train other people, like my old trainer did. That's the one thing I still miss—the shows," Ava added.

U

Once she'd started middle school, Tally noticed, people didn't ask her what she wanted to be when she grew up as much. That seemed like a question reserved for little kids. Then again, she knew she'd have to pick a major in college—she'd heard Isabelle talking about that at the barn.

"Think you'll ever come back to riding?" Jacob asked.

Ava shook her head no. "I love gymnastics too much, and it's such a big commitment. I don't really have time for a second sport. Oh, but I just heard that Danny's doing super well with his new owner. He isn't stopping at all now!"

"Danny was...tricky," Tally said with a grin. Danny, or Stonelea Dance Party in the show ring, was the very first catch-ride she'd gotten from Ryan. When she took him to a horse show, he stopped and she fell off at the very first jump. "His new rider must be really good," she added.

"Well, he's such a one-person pony," Ava said thoughtfully. "You rode him when I was going to sell him, and he had a bunch of different riders at the time. I bet if it was just the two of you it would have been different."

CHAPTER 18

Tally was wrapping up her shift on the school aisle on Saturday morning when she heard Ryan's booming voice in the small indoor. Situated in the middle of the two aisles at the Quince Oaks barn, this ring was smaller than the big indoor ring at the top of the hill. Tally learned how spoiled she was when she first started going to horse shows with Ryan. The Oaks' small indoor was pretty close in size to the show rings at other barns.

Tally topped off the water bucket in Lil Bit's stall, the last one on the school aisle next to the stairs that led up to the office. She could hear Ryan from all the way around the corner and decided to watch the rest of his lesson before packing up to meet her mom.

After giving Lil a quick pat and latching her stall

door, Tally wrapped the hose around its holder under the stairs. She plucked her gloves out of her pockets and pulled them on as she walked around to the ring and took a seat on the chilly bleachers. Maggie and Mac were taking a lesson with Ryan. Sparkles' breath was coming out in little frosty puffs from her nose, and Tally pulled the hood of her jacket up over her hat. As soon as she stopped working on a winter shift, she felt a whole lot colder.

"Okay, Maggie, let's do your single plank on the diagonal off your left lead, then around to your outside line in four strides, diagonal in five, and end on your other outside four-stride. This ring is very similar in size to the one you'll be showing in a few weeks from now, so it's good practice to get used to the lines. Take your *time* with the changes."

Mac halted in the corner just past Tally to watch Maggie jump around. Ryan encouraged the girls to watch each other lesson, but he had a strict no-chatting policy until they were walking and cooling out. Mac had her back to Tally in the corner as Maggie and Pete got started.

Maggie took her time bending Pete to the inside

and lifting her eyes before asking the horse for his left lead canter.

"*Good*, Maggie. Now you're thinking about it and asking definitively. Keep your pace the same as you approach this single."

Maggie and Pete rounded the far corner and turned to the green plank jump. Maggie shifted her hands left through the turn as Tally had been practicing, too. Pete's pace slowed as they got closer to the single jump.

"Nope, that's the pony stride!" called Ryan. "Circle and try again. Leave his mouth alone, remember? You're covering more ground on a horse, and your eye needs to adjust. If you let go and just flow out of the corner, you'll find a better distance."

Tally watched Maggie's face as they came out of the turn again. She was relieved to see that Maggie didn't look upset—just focused.

One, two, one, two, one, Tally counted in her mind as Maggie and Pete found a better spot for the plank.

"There it is! Now, do the same thing coming to your first line. Count the rhythm, let go with your hands and just stay the same," said Ryan.

Maggie shifted her hands right for the next turn

and found a good spot into the line.

"Leg on...maintain..." Ryan instructed her. Pete met the oxer out of the line just right.

"Nice! Keep it just like this, Mags."

Maggie came out of the corner for the five-stride diagonal line and Pete's pace noticeably changed. They chipped in to the vertical.

"That's okay, keep riding," Ryan said. Pete jumped out of the line in five strides. "You're leaning. You're *leaning*!" said Ryan, as Pete missed the change behind as they headed for their last line. Maggie quickly brought Pete down to the trot and then asked again for the left lead.

"Good fix, now just flow."

Maggie and Pete found a nice jump into the outside line and flowed for four strides. It looked like Pete made an extra effort over the oxer out.

"Atta girl, Maggie," said Ryan. "You just got a little disorganized at your diagonal line so you pulled and found the pony stride in, right?" Maggie nodded. "And then because you were still feeling disorganized, you cut your turn and leaned rather than sitting up and riding straight to the corner for your change.

But the rest was spot-on. You should be really proud, kiddo. You've made a lot of progress already. Let Pete quit with that."

Maggie let her reins out and rubbed Pete's neck. Tally could see her talking to him as they passed the in-gate.

Ryan raised the jumps on the outside line and then walked over to the other. "You'll do the same course in just a minute here, Mac," said Ryan. "Remember to take each jump one at a time. Wipe your mental slate clean for each one. If you have a big, strong jump in to a line, you'll have to squeeze your fingers and balance on the way out. But on the next line, maybe you'll jump in with less pony. Then you'll want to softly move up, right? Whatever happens on course, you need a fresh start approaching each new jump. Okay, go ahead."

Mac's head swiveled around and Tally could tell she was going over the course in her mind. From the walk, Sparkles stepped right into a big, rocking canter.

"No more pony than that," said Ryan.

Sparkles jumped the single plank beautifully and found a great spot jumping in to the first line. Mac seemed to take back a little bit over their four strides and met the oxer at a long-ish, gappy distance.

"Why are you pulling?" asked Ryan. "Let go in the line if you jump in well, because you've already covered some ground jumping in. Keep the canter the same."

Mac turned left and jumped the vertical of the diagonal line. Tally saw her slow down again.

"Keep flowing!" Ryan called. Mac let go of the reins and Sparkles smoothly moved up to meet the oxer out.

"Let the reins out a bit, I want a loop in there. Good," said Ryan. "Now do this last line that way. No pulling."

Down the final line, Mac sat up tall and they easily found their oxer out of the line in four.

"Did you feel that? Without the reins to pull, you used your body to keep that steady canter," Ryan told Mac, who nodded enthusiastically. "*Really* good. We'll just keep working on your instinct to pull down the lines. There's still that muscle memory leftover from Joey. But this is the same concept as leaving the previous jump in the past and taking one jump at a time, right? You have to ride the pony you've got underneath you."

U

"This pony has got a softer mouth," Ryan added. "So when you say whoa, he's going to *whoa*. And you don't need that. All you need to do if you jump in well is to stay the same. If you find a deeper or a longer spot at the vertical jumping into the line, *then* you adjust. We'll work more on staying the same some more in your next lesson. Great riding. Both of you. Let those ponies walk a few laps and throw their coolers on in their stalls, please."

"Thanks, Ryan," both Mac and Maggie said in unison and then giggled at their timing.

"You're welcome, nice work," Ryan said, and then looked in Tally's direction.

"Tal, meet me in the tack room in ten minutes?"

CHAPTER 19

Tally got up from the bleachers and made a left for the boarder aisle, only to see her mom walking into the barn. She glanced at her watch—12:24 p.m.

"Hey, Mom," she said, catching up to her mother on the aisle. "I thought we said one o'clock today?"

"Tally, hi! Yes, we did, but Ryan asked me to meet him here at 12:30."

Tally felt a flutter in her stomach. *They were both meeting with Ryan? What was this about?* Then she saw her dad trailing behind her mother.

"Nothing to worry about. It's a good meeting," her dad said. Then he pointed to the tricolor Tally had hung on Cam's door. She had the perfect spot for it in her bedroom but wanted to celebrate their first show together by displaying it on his stall for a while first.

"Tally up the ribbons!" her dad said.

Tally smiled. Corny as it was, she loved her dad's play on her name.

"Did you label it?" he asked. Tally's dad always encouraged her to label every ribbon with the date, venue, and a note or two about the class so she could always look back on the show memories. That applied to both the top ribbons...and to the lower ones that Tally would sooner forget.

"Of course," Tally said with a grin.

She led her parents over to Cam's stall and gave them carrots to feed him while they waited. Then Ryan rounded the corner at the other end of the aisle.

"Hey, Harts," he said, grinning broadly and gesturing toward the tack room. "Step into my office."

Tally followed her parents inside as they took seats on Field Ridge director's chairs across from Ryan. Tally sat down on Mac's tack trunk.

"So. James and Stacy, you know what this is all about, but Tally does not, correct?" Ryan asked, grinning at her parents.

Her mom and dad nodded.

"Would you like to do the honors?"

Tally's mom turned from Ryan to Tally. "Ryan has a really special horse show opportunity for you," her mother began. "Your dad and I would like for you to take it, but only as long as your teachers will work with you to get your assignments done and you take any school work with you that's needed."

"Yes, of course I will. What's the show?" Tally asked. It felt like time had shifted and everything was moving in slow motion. All three of the adults had huge smiles.

"It's in Florida, Tal," said Ryan. "Do you want to show Cam down there after Thanksgiving?"

Tally looked from Ryan to her parents and back to Ryan again. "*Florida*? I get to show Cam in *Florida*?"

Her dad chuckled as Ryan nodded. "Yup. I'm going down for a couple of weeks to try horses for some clients. I figured it would be a good opportunity to bring a few horses down too, and go to the show near the Gulf Coast. The weather will be great, and it'll be a nice break from the cold for you and Cam. What do you think?"

"Thank you! Oh my gosh, I can't believe it. So, this is during school?" Tally asked.

"Yes, which is why we need to check in with your teachers. You'd fly down on a Wednesday and back on Sunday, so it's three school days," said Tally's mom. Her dad put his hand on her arm.

"I'm sure it will work out fine with your teachers," her dad interjected. "We'll just make sure when we talk to them on Monday. Mac is going too, so we'll set it up for you two to fly down together. It's a considerable expense, but it's such a good opportunity that your mother and I will make it a big Christmas present for you, and Ryan said you can work off the rest in Florida, okay?"

"You'll help Lupe water the horses, filling hay nets, tacking and untacking horses, cleaning tack…that kind of thing," Ryan added.

"Great!" Tally said. "I can't wait. I'm so excited. Thank you, Ryan!"

"And?" her dad asked with a laugh.

"I wasn't done! Thank you, Dad. Thank you, Mom. This is the best present ever."

CHAPTER 20

That Thursday was Thanksgiving and Tally was feeling *very* thankful. And nervous, and excited, and like she wished time would move a little faster! Tally and her parents always drove to her grandparents' house an hour away for Thanksgiving, and her aunt and uncle met them there as well.

While the adults had cocktails and appetizers, Tally slipped out to the covered porch off the back of the house to call Mac.

"Hey, are you having the best Thanksgiving ever?" Mac asked dryly. "Because I am. I love having twenty-eight cousins in my house."

Tally laughed. "At least you have other kids there. I'm the only one."

"True," Mac replied. "How are we going to make it

until Wednesday? After today that's…five whole days until we leave."

"I *know*. I'm going to pack tomorrow I think! Hey, so I was so excited I didn't even think to ask Ryan—which horses are going to Florida besides Sparkles and Cam?"

"There's four. Wait, hang on a second." The phone got muffled as Mac called something out and then returned to the phone. "I have to run in just a minute. Something about football. Anyway, it's Sparkles, Cam, Isabelle's junior hunter Pip, and Maestro, the dark bay at the end of the aisle by the indoor ring."

"Oh yeah, he's really cute. Who owns him?" Tally asked.

"A woman named Suzette—she's friends with Cam's owner, Pia, actually. She shows in the Adults, too. Ugh, I have to go, everyone's yelling for me now. I'll call you tomorrow when I'm packing."

Tally said goodbye to her friend and stared out the porch windows at the bare trees blowing in the wind. *Florida*. Tally had never been before, and she'd only seen horse show photos from the winter circuits. Actually, she'd never even seen a palm tree in real life before! She hoped she wouldn't feel out of place at such a big show so far from home.

When her family began slowing down on their Thanksgiving meal, it was time for the annual tradition of everyone sharing what they were thankful for that year. This year was easy for Tally.

"I am thankful for my parents allowing me to show in Florida, and for all the amazing riding opportunities I've been getting," Tally said. Her father beamed and her grandparents, aunt, and uncle all looked happy for her, and maybe a little confused.

"You've gotten really serious about your horseback riding, haven't you, sweetheart?" asked her grandma.

Tally nodded her head yes.

"That's wonderful, dear. It's so fulfilling to find something you love this much."

The next day, Tally carefully folded up three pairs of tan breeches, a pair of navy schooling breeches, three show shirts, one short sleeve workout top, a sweatshirt, a pair of pajamas, and her show jacket, tucking them neatly into her carry-on suitcase. Then she went to her drawers and pulled out enough underwear and boot socks for her four days of riding, plus an extra pair of each, just in case.

Ryan had emailed her parents the details: Tally would take a lesson on her arrival day, Wednesday. Then, she would have a warmup day in the show ring on Thursday. On Friday, she would flat Cam and take a tour of the show grounds. And finally, her division—the Low Children's Hunters—would run across Saturday and Sunday. It was the most riding she'd ever done in a short period of time, and Tally could *not* wait.

The rest of Friday and Saturday crawled along at a painfully slow pace, and then on Sunday, she was due at the barn by noon to help get the horses ready to ship. Following instructions from Isabelle, she gave each of the four horses a thorough grooming, and then helped put stable sheets on them—matching plaid blankets that looked tidy and fancy, Tally thought. The horses' trip south would take a full day, including stops for water and to replenish their hay. Ryan had hired a professional shipping company to take the horses to Florida, while he and Lupe drove the Field Ridge trailer down with supplies a day earlier, in order to set up at the show stalls.

"The shippers called Brenna and said they will be here in about forty-five minutes," Isabelle said. "Thanks for all your help, Tally. Brenna and I will make sure the right horses get loaded onto the truck," she added with a little laugh.

"Okay! When are you getting to Florida?" Tally asked.

"I fly down on Tuesday. We're going to try horses in the afternoon Tuesday and then some more on Wednesday morning. How about you?"

"Mac and I get in Wednesday afternoon," Tally said. "I've never done a winter circuit before, I still can't really believe it."

"Well, this technically isn't a winter circuit," Isabelle explained. "That starts in January. But this horse show is so popular they added some December dates as well. I think our week is called the Season Kickoff since it begins on the first day of the new show season, December 1."

"Oh, okay, that makes sense. Well, whatever, it's winter and we're going to be warm so I don't really care what it's called," Tally said with a laugh.

"Exactly!" said Isabelle. "It's like bonus time in Florida. Pip loves it down there. You and Cam will, too."

Tally smiled. "Are you selling Pip to buy a new horse?"

"No, we're not selling Pip. I'm actually going to move up from the three-three Small Juniors to the three-six Small Juniors on him," said Isabelle. "We're shopping in Florida for a jumper for me that my sister can also ride when I leave for college."

Tally recalled seeing Isabelle's younger sister Louisa around the barn, but they hadn't taken lessons together yet.

"So, the trip is horse shopping for you and showing Pip also?"

"Yup. My first time in the three-six!" I can't wait."

"Me neither," said Tally, grinning broadly. "I even set a countdown clock on my phone!"

"I love it. Well, I'm going to check in with Brenna. I'll see you down there!"

Tally said goodbye to Isabelle and then slipped into Cam's stall. She stood at his chest and scratched around his ears. It was always so sweet and peaceful to spend time with him. Tally dug into her coat pocket for a peppermint and Cam made adorable nickering sounds as she did.

♘

"Hold on, hold on, I'm going as fast as I can," said Tally with a laugh. Cam gobbled up the mint and Tally gave him a strong hug around his neck. "Travel safe, buddy. I can't wait to see you in a few days."

· CHAPTER 21 ·

The flight attendant dug underneath a pile of pretzels and pulled out two packages of cookies, then placed them on Tally and Mac's trays.

"I knew I had a couple more hiding in there," she said. "Just hit the button if you girls need anything else."

Tally and Mac thanked her and then Tally resumed staring out the window at the clouds. It still didn't feel real. She and her best friend were on their way to show their horses in Florida. And on a school day!

Mac gasped softly at the horror movie she was watching on her phone. Tally turned over the dog-eared page of her novel and settled back into her seat.

Just over an hour later, the girls were descending the elevator at the airport in Florida, practically bouncing up and down with excitement. Ryan was on the lower level with Suzette, waiting to drive to the show grounds. He waved when he saw them.

"How was your flight?" he asked as a giggling Tally and Mac bounded up to him.

"Good!" Tally said.

"We're ready to ride," Mac added, gesturing to their boots and breeches.

"I see this, very nice," Ryan told them. "Tally, Mac, you know Suzette, right?"

"I haven't met Tally yet," said Suzette, smiling warmly at her. "Nice to meet you. And good to see you too, Mac."

On the drive to the show grounds, Tally felt like she was a little kid again, trying to hold it together in the back seat. Everything Mac said to her was somehow hilarious and it was all she could to do to keep from laughing hysterically—the kind of laughter where you can't control yourself and what starts out as funny just ends up awkward and embarrassing.

The half hour drive to the showgrounds flew by as Mac and Tally chatted about every horse they knew in the barn and just about every horse show they'd ever been to.

♘

"I'm not sure I've heard them stop to take a breath," Suzette joked to Ryan at one point.

When he turned the truck onto Fox Lane, Ryan cleared his throat.

"Almost here, girls," he said. "Lupe should have your horses ready by the time we pull in. You'll get right on to lesson, okay?

Tally and Mac nodded, finally taking in their surroundings. The entrance to the showgrounds was lined with palm trees, tucked in with skinny pines and bigger shade trees.

They turned left at the entrance, greeted by a rustic looking sign: "Copper Top Farm." Ryan slowed the truck, which was kicking up plenty of dust as they rolled down the dirt road entrance. The right side of the dirt road was lined with turnouts, small fenced paddocks with trees in the corners, including those palm trees that kept making Tally smile. She felt very far from home, but in the best way.

Just past the shady paddocks, a show ring came into view.

"This is one of the main hunter rings—you'll show here, Tally," said Ryan. Mac kicked Tally's foot with her own as the girls gazed out at the jumps. Tally noticed the standards shaped like candy canes that she'd seen in horse show photos, but never in person. Then Ryan turned right down a wider dirt road. On their left was the biggest paddock they'd seen, with a big black horse grazing underneath a tree, and a little black pony at his side. A sign directed them straight toward barns 1 and 2.

"This is home for the week," said Ryan as the blue and white tents came into view. The Field Ridge banner and Ryan's director's chairs were set up at the opening to an aisle of stalls. The ground was covered in mulch and baskets of flowers lined the entryway.

"Fancy," Tally whispered to Mac, who nodded in return.

Ryan parked the truck in front of the aisle and Tally spotted Cam on a set of cross ties just inside their stall area. The girls grabbed their backpacks and bounded out of the truck.

"Hi, Cam!" Tally greeted the handsome gelding, who raised his head when he saw her. She wrapped up his neck in a hug.

"Tally, you made it." Tally turned to see Lupe.

"Hi!" she said as he placed a square pad and a half pad on Cam's back. "Thank you for tacking him," she added.

Lupe gave her a thumbs-up and Tally put her bag down on a little folding table to pull out her helmet and gloves as she saw Mac doing.

"You girls will get to lesson in your show ring today," said Ryan. "They had some classes in it but now it's open for schooling. It's a nice perk at this show," he added. "Suzette will join you, too."

Ten minutes later, everyone was tacked, mounted, and walking away from the barn on their horses. Ryan directed them down a sandy path outside of a huge grass field.

"You'll flat in here on Friday," Ryan told the group. "It's sandy underneath the grass, so it's a nice, forgiving footing for the horses."

Tally felt like she was in a dream. The showgrounds were beautiful, and the jumpers schooling with their riders in the grass field looked like something straight out of a movie.

The group walked past a mobile tack shop, a dining area, some photo op set-ups, and then the Grand Prix ring, directly across from the grass field. In it, a gray horse sailed through a triple combination of yellow and white rails. He stretched to clear the third element, an imposing oxer, and the spectators in the covered pavilion whooped and hollered as he galloped away.

"And that's a clear round, with a time of fifty-nine point two four seconds," said the announcer. Cam perked his ears in that direction.

"Exciting, huh buddy?" Tally said as she rubbed his withers. "I'm excited, too."

CHAPTER 22

The group arrived at the show ring Tally had seen on their way in, labeled "Hunter Ring Two" with a big sign just outside the fence line. A warm-up area was right next to the show ring, and Ryan directed the riders that way.

"They're still watering and dragging the ring, so let's start trotting around here."

In front of her, Suzette cued Maestro into a trot. Tally and Cam followed, with Mac and Sparkles behind them. The schooling area was sandwiched between the show ring and some small fenced paddocks. Cam was very interested in the pony who was turned out right next to them.

"Keep his focus on what you're doing, Tal," Ryan said to her and Tally put her inside leg on and squeezed her inside rein. Cam didn't seem to notice and craned his neck toward the pony.

"You can be a little tough on him there, Tal. He's a good boy but he still needs some schooling from time to time," said Ryan. Tally put her inside spur into Cam's side a bit and applied more pressure on the inside rein. Cam dropped his head and engaged from behind.

After the group trotted in both directions, the show ring was done and the three riders walked through the in-gate. Ryan thanked the driver of the truck dragging the ring and directed his students to canter.

Cam tossed his head and picked up a big, bouncy canter underneath her. He seemed as excited about Florida as she was. Tally added leg to get him to move forward, rather than up and down, and Cam willingly covered more ground. Tally's legs felt a little wobbly and the lesson felt like a blur as Ryan asked them to follow one another over a single birch jump set on a diagonal. Then, one by one, they jumped the outside line in five strides, followed by a diagonal line in six.

"The lines are flowing, so land and just maintain leg," Ryan told Tally as they jumped in to the diagonal. "That's the ride," he added as they jumped out.

Before Tally even really felt like they were taking a lesson, the group was walking back to the barn.

"It's really pretty here, huh?" said Suzette, riding beside her. Maestro, a beautiful dark bay with stripe and snip, stretched his neck out long as Suzette held the buckle of the reins.

"So pretty," Tally said with a nod. "I still can't believe I got off a plane and got right on a horse."

Suzette laughed. "It's super different from riding at home. You just kinda go with the flow here."

The group retraced their path back to the barn and Ryan directed them to dismount between the trucks parked in front of the Field Ridge aisle.

"Lupe will show you how we untack here at the show setup," Ryan told Tally as she swung down from the saddle and ran up her stirrups.

"Lead him straight in here and then carefully turn around," Lupe told her. It was a tight space in the grooming stall, but Cam didn't seem to mind. "Grab his saddle and pads and you can stick them right on that rack," added Lupe, who took off Cam's bridle and slipped on his halter in one smooth movement.

An hour later, Tally had untacked Cam, Maestro,

and Sparkles, brushing them and picking out their feet before returning them to their show stalls. The huge tent over the stalls reminded Tally of going to the circus with her parents as a little kid. The horses seemed to be as settled as they were at home.

"Thanks for your help, Tal," Ryan said, hanging a bridle from a hook at the front of their setup. A bucket of water was secured against a wide fence post and Ryan dunked a sponge into it as he worked on the bridle.

"Sure," said Tally. "I was just thinking the horses seem so relaxed here."

"Well, we got them settled in on Monday," Ryan said.

"Still, it's so different from home," Tally added, latching Maestro's stall door.

"Show horses," Suzette told her with a warm smile. "They're used to it, and they tend to settle in fast. Amazing, right?"

Tally nodded. It really was.

That night, Mac polished her boots at the hotel room desk while Tally set out her toothbrush and phone charger in the bathroom.

"What classes do we have tomorrow?" asked Mac.

"You're asking me?" Tally answered with a little laugh. "I still feel like we landed on another planet!"

Mac smiled as she buffed the toe of her boot with a soft brush. "I forget that you've only done this a few times. You seem like such a pro now."

"I think this is my...fifth rated show? Maybe the sixth?" said Tally. "But flying on a plane to get here and taking a lesson like, the moment we get to the show grounds was brand new."

"Yeah, travel shows can be crazy."

"Anyway, I have no idea what classes we're showing in tomorrow except that Ryan called it our warm-up day," said Tally. On the desk next to Mac's boot-cleaning supplies, her phone chirped and vibrated, moving it across the surface. Tally answered it, eager to catch her mom and dad up on her first day in Florida.

CHAPTER 23

The hotel room alarm clock went off at 6:15 a.m. Both Tally and Mac fumbled in the dark to try to turn it off and find the light.

Mac's sheets rustled as she got up and walked to the bathroom, while Tally stayed in her bed for a moment with her eyes closed. She imagined herself and Cam in Hunter Ring Two, finding all of their distances.

The girls got ready mostly in silence. Tally opened the mini fridge and pulled out a yogurt parfait and an orange juice that Ryan had picked up at the grocery store on their way to the hotel the night before.

"Is it any good?" Mac asked as Tally started on her yogurt at the desk.

"Actually, it is good," Tally said. "Do you know why I'm eating it now, while it's still dark outside?"

"No, why?" asked Mac, her words muffled by the toothbrush in her mouth.

"Because I spill everything on my show clothes."

Mac walked over to the sink and spit. "Ha! I do the same thing," she said. "I'll eat with you in my pajamas."

By 7:45, Mac and Tally were pulling into the showgrounds with Isabelle. Ryan and Suzette had arrived earlier since Suzette's ring started at eight, while Tally and Mac's ring would get going at nine.

The girls all climbed out of the car. Tally zipped up her jacket. It was considerably warmer here than at home, but still chilly by Florida standards. Some people even had heavy coats and scarves on, she noticed. In the two grooming stalls stood Cam and Sparkles, both in their stable sheets, both looking adorable.

"Good morning!" Mac said in a sing-songy voice, scratching her pony behind the ears. In the next open grooming stall over, Cam stomped an oiled hoof, as if eager for attention, too.

"I didn't forget you, buddy," said Tally, giving the horse a peppermint from the bowl on the table. He licked her hand when he was done and Tally noticed that the butterflies in her stomach were starting early.

Isabelle and Mac were standing at the white board to the right of the grooming stalls, so Tally gave Cam's shoulder a quick pat and joined them. Ryan had a little grid written out on the board with places to put a check for grooming, braiding, and each horse's division. Suzette and Maestro were doing the Adult Equitation in Hunter 1 this morning. Tally and Mac were down for the warmup classes set at 2'6," while Isabelle would show in the 3' warm up rounds for her first day in Florida.

"Lupe just texted," Isabelle told the girls. "The two-six division is going first in Hunter 2 so you guys should get ready."

Tally felt like her heart was going to leap out of her body.

Why was she this nervous to show?

After Tally and Mac put on their boots, show jackets, helmets, and gloves, Lupe arrived back at the stalls. "You ready for your horses?" he asked them.

"Yup," Mac said, adjusting her hairnet underneath her helmet. She was the picture of cool and calm. Tally practically felt like she'd never ridden a horse before.

Lupe swapped Cam's show halter for his bridle and

gave his face a quick swipe with a rag. He handed the reins to Tally, who walked over to the step ladder that served as a mounting block just outside their stalls. Mac was right behind her.

"You okay, Tally? You're so quiet."

"Just nervous, I guess," said Tally as the girls turned left to head for the rings.

"Don't be nervous. This is such a nice, laid back show. And it's your warm-up day before our divisions this weekend."

Tally's mind raced as they walked toward the ring together. She suddenly longed for the days of the Quince Oaks Schooling Series. Those shows were just fun. This one felt totally different for some reason.

Mac was chatting about some friends at school and Tally tried her best to pay attention. But her mind kept wandering back to her first show with Cam. How they did so well and were champion their first time out. Could she repeat that here?

As Mac and Tally passed Hunter 1 on the way to their ring, Ryan waved from the warmup area adjacent to it. "I'll be there in five minutes. You can start walking and trotting in your warmup ring," he called to them.

♘

Mac and Tally read the course diagrams outside of the ring and recited the course aloud a couple of times. The warmup ring for Hunter 2 was empty except for two adults chatting in the middle so Mac walked Sparkles beside Tally and Cam.

"You know what I just realized?" asked Mac. "Well, I just realized two things, actually. One, Cameron doesn't have a fancy show name. He's just Cameron! I guess when you're this perfect, you don't need more than one name. Right, cutie?" she said, leaning toward Cam.

Tally forced a smile.

"And the other thing I realized is that 'Cam' is 'Mac,' spelled backwards!"

The girls made eye contact and then doubled over laughing. It was just the comic relief that Tally needed.

"Deep thoughts with Mac Bennett this morning?" she asked her friend.

"Well *you* didn't notice," Mac teased her back. "Come on, let's start trotting around."

Tally's nerves came back as she began warming up Cameron.

"Hip angle, Tally," said Ryan as he approached the

warmup ring for Hunter 2. "You're a little behind the motion. There you go, that's better. See how he's more willing to go forward when you close your hip angle?"

Mac popped over the center jump in both directions and then the oxer on the right side. "You're good to go," Ryan said. "Tally, you come again. You turned too early down there and that's why you found the jump on the half stride. Stay out longer, okay?"

It took another couple of tries before Tally found a good distance to her warmup jump. She felt disconnected while watching her friend's first round in the show ring. Everything about Florida felt different. For the first time, she just wanted to get her rounds over with.

"Ready, Tal? Know your course?" Ryan asked as Mac brought Sparkles down to the trot for their closing circle after their first round.

Tally nodded.

"Make sure you carry a good pace to that first jump, and you can look for your turn early, but don't *make* the turn early. Take a deep breath and have fun out there."

♘

Tally walked through the in-gate and then immediately picked up the trot, her strategy planned with Ryan to show off Cam's best gait. She took her time asking for his tricky right lead, and kept her leg on to get up to ring pace. On the short side of the ring, she felt Cam pop up behind. *What was that about?*

Tally sat and rode him forward. Cam hopped up again and flicked his ears back. Tally tried to be patient for the first turn but could tell she'd made it too early. She straightened Cam out the best she could and found a tight distance to that first vertical. As she passed the in-gate on their way to the first line, Ryan's voice was low and measured.

"Take a deep breath and relax," he told Tally. "Just let Cam do his job."

Tally waited a stride or two before turning Cam to the outside line and found a decent distance in. She put her leg on for the out, only noticing by stride four that she had plenty of horse. She tried collecting Cam but they were deep to the oxer and he rubbed the rail on the jump out.

Tally felt discombobulated for the remainder of the course. It was like she either had too much pace or not enough and Cam always seemed to hop at the ends of the ring. When Tally and Cam walked out, Ryan was talking to Mac about their next course. He sent her in and then turned to Tally. "Sit tight for just a minute here and we'll talk about it, Tal."

CHAPTER 24

Lupe, Suzette, and Isabelle had arrived in time to watch Mac's second trip, and the group burst into applause as she landed off the single oxer to end her course. Ryan clapped hard and then turned to Tally.

"Okay, so, I want you to try something in this next round," he said. "I want you to try smiling."

"What, like, when I come out of the ring?" Tally asked.

"No, while you're *in* the ring," said Ryan. "You're riding a little stiff today, which is not the norm for you. That's why Cam is hopping at the ends of the ring. Your body is stiff and you're driving him forward with your seat and, sometimes, too much leg. Like in the line where you rubbed the oxer, right?"

Tally nodded.

"That's why I'm asking you to smile. Smiling forces you to relax your body. Do it when you feel tense, or anytime you think of it, really."

Tally felt herself relax a little even when he said that. Figuring out why Cam was behaving this way was a good start.

"You can also count your 'one, two, one, two' out loud if you'd like. Whispering it to yourself will also force you to breathe. It's just another horse show, Tally, try not to let the idea of it being Florida get into your head."

"Okay," she said.

"Winning is great, but making sure you're having fun is the top priority. That's why we do this, right?" said Ryan, giving Cam a pat. The rider who went in after Mac was now coming out.

"You remember this trip? Yellow flowers, outside line in five, single oxer, judge's line, diagonal in six?"

Tally nodded again.

"Try it right now. Smile," Ryan said. Tally felt herself turning red as she forced a grin and took a breath.

"See? Your whole body just changed and so did Cam's expression. I don't care how silly it feels. Think about smiling as often as you possibly can during this trip. And have *fun*," he added.

Tally and Cam were on the short side of the ring, about to turn to the first jump when she felt his body tense, like he wanted to hop again. So, she smiled. A big, dumb, goofy smile. Cam instantly relaxed. They turned toward their first jump and Tally kept smiling. It was almost a nice reminder from her face to her brain that this *was* fun. Cam *was* a good boy. She might as well enjoy the ride.

The second trip went a whole lot better than the first. Tally relaxed enough that she actually had time to think on course. As they approached the single oxer, it occurred to Tally that the last few horses and ponies she rode might have found it spooky and tried to suck back. On Cameron, all the jumps were all kind of the same. In a good way.

"Well, that was a heck of a lot better," said Ryan as Tally came out of the ring. She was still smiling. "He didn't hop once because you relaxed your body, and you kept breathing, right? I'm proud of you, Tal, way to turn that around. Why don't you hop down so Lupe can take off Cam's martingale for the hack?"

Tally dismounted and looked away from Ryan. She felt that familiar, about-to-cry feeling bubbling up and wanted so badly to push it back down.

"We've got six more horses with two trips each before we go under saddle," the announcer said. "I only have two of you checked in. If you're doing the two-foot-six in Hunter Ring Two, I need you to check in with me now."

Tally hoped the announcer interrupted the moment but Ryan still noticed that Tally was avoiding making eye contact.

"What's going on?" he asked. Tally recognized the overly upbeat tone Ryan used when he was trying to make someone feel better.

"I guess...I don't know, I guess I just felt like everyone expected us to be champion again," said Tally, staring down at the polished toes of her boots, now speckled with sandy footing.

"One second," said Ryan. "Lupe, you'll get Pip ready for the three-foot? Thanks. Come walk over here with me, Tally."

Tally followed Ryan, who double checked that Cameron's girth was loose before leading him over to a tree at the edge of the warmup ring by the road. The sun had come out in full force now so they stood in the shade.

"I wish you'd told me how you were feeling before that first trip," he said.

"So that I could have ridden it better?" Tally asked.

"No!" said Ryan with a kind laugh. "So that you wouldn't have put this pressure on yourself. Listen, when you've got a horse like this one, you have to forget about what people say—how Cam is perfect and he's a total packer and all of that. All that's going to do is put pressure on you. But there's no need to add pressure. Like I said, winning is great, but pre-serving the fun is the top priority."

"Thanks," Tally said softly. "It's really different having a horse that could do well every time we go in the ring. I guess it does feel like a lot of pressure."

"Listen, since Cam is a packer, he can show you the ropes. But that still doesn't mean you're a shoe-in to win every class or be champion every time. There are so many factors, Tal. He's a great horse but he's not everyone's cup of tea. Judges can have a 'type,' or a way of going that they prefer and Cam may or may not be it. You can have the trip of your life and get a low ribbon because you've got super high-quality horses in your ring, with good riders who are nailing their trips. Or, you can have an okay trip and win everything. It depends on the day, the judge, the other people...or the way the wind is blowing. There are too many factors to count. We are focused on improvement and consistency. And the only way to get more consistent is with miles. Each time you show, you gain more miles. Know what I mean?"

Tally nodded, smiling. There was definitely something really cool about gaining these miles in the sun at a gorgeous farm in Florida

"I can tell the smiling in the ring is helping," Ryan added.

"Yeah, I was thinking about our first show together when I heard the announcer say our names. I couldn't stop smiling when I heard that."

"Well there you go," said Ryan. "Think of that. Think about how many people want you to ride their horses, and that you get to show at a place like this."

Tally nodded, taking it in.

"Proud of you, kiddo. Let's prioritize the fun for

this week, huh?" Ryan handed Tally Cam's reins. "Hang out and watch and you can get on for the hack after a few more horses jump. Your next job is to have fun in the under saddle class."

· CHAPTER 25 ·

Tally's smile in the ring during the hack was a genuine one. Cam seemed very happy to open up his trot and show off, and Tally noticed the judge watching him.

"Slow your post down a little," Ryan told her as she trotted past the in-gate. "Better."

When they cantered, Tally got up out of the tack a little bit and kept Cameron on the quarter line to keep him visible to the judge. It seemed like a longer hack class to Tally, and she wondered if it was a difficult choice for the judge to order such a nice group of horses.

The class lined up and Cam was called in third. Tally beamed as they collected their yellow ribbon. After pinning the under saddle, the announcer called the results of the over fences classes. Sparkles and Mac were second in both classes, while Cam and Tally were seventh and fourth.

Tally offered to help Lupe untack and cool out the horses at the barn, but Ryan wanted her to stay with Mac to watch Isabelle show.

"I have plenty more work for you to do later on," Ryan said. "Enjoy cheering on your teammate in her division, okay?"

Tally and Mac sat on a picnic table to watch Isabelle's three-foot warmup division.

"The jumps only went up in height by two holes— why do they look so much bigger?" Tally wondered out loud.

"I know. I didn't think it was so noticeable going from two-six to two-nine. But two holes definitely makes a difference," said Mac. "Isabelle makes it look easy though, you'll see."

Mac was right. Isabelle was first in the ring for the three-foot division, and she and Pip looked relaxed as could be as he floated down the lines.

That afternoon, Tally helped Lupe with turning out the horses and bathing them afterward. Cam would go out first, and Ryan said they'd stand at the gate for a bit, just to make sure he didn't act too silly, since he wasn't used to being out by himself—at home he went out in a group of four.

The turnout was a half-moon shape, and since the footing was just sand, not the grass that their horses were used to at home, Ryan brought a flake of hay for Cam. Tally took off Cam's halter and shut the gate. Ryan stood beside her as they watched the horse explore his new surroundings.

Cam gazed off into the distance at first and then trotted the length of the small turnout before sniffing around in the sand.

"Pretty different from the turnout back home, huh, buddy?" Ryan asked.

Cam bent his knees and laid down for a roll. With all four feet in the air, it looked like he was smiling. Then he stood up, shook off the sand, and wandered over to the hay to eat.

"Oh, he's wild all right," Ryan joked. "Stay for another few minutes, Tal, and then you can head back to the barn. It's good for the horses to have this time to themselves, to have some autonomy and make their own decisions."

"Because they spend so much time in their stalls at a horse show?" Tally asked.

"Exactly. It's important to give them time to just be a horse whenever possible."

Tally watched Cam eat for a few more minutes and then walked back to the stalls, looking back over her shoulder a couple of times to check on him. Cam swished his tail and dug into his hay.

Tally spent the rest of the day cleaning tack and swapping horses in and out of the turnout. She bathed Cam and Sparkles while Lupe took Maestro and Pip. She and Mac walked over to the jumper ring to watch for a while, and then they decided to take their horses out to hand graze.

Lupe put scrims on each of them—Sparkles wore a scrim embroidered with "Bennett" while Cam's read "Field Ridge." Tally asked about the standing wraps on both horses.

"It's to reduce any swelling and provide support after a day of showing, since they are standing in their stalls. Not like going out at night when they are home," Lupe explained. "Doing the wraps takes some practice, but I'll show you how to do it."

♘

Tally thanked him—she learned something new about horse care every time she worked with Lupe—and followed Mac out of the stalls and over to the grass field. Cam sniffed around for quite some time before finding an acceptable place to graze.

"Sparkles is a lot less picky," Mac joked as her pony nibbled away at the short grass.

"I think Cam isn't sure what to make of the sand underneath," said Tally. "You normally can't pick his head up from grazing!"

The girls talked about their day and did a video call with Maggie back home.

"Hi, Cam. Hi, Mr. Sparklepants!" she greeted them.

"How's it going there?" Mac asked.

"Good," said Maggie. "You know the trainer Nicole from the riding school? Ryan set us up to take some lessons with her until he gets back, since it will be two full weeks between the show and horse shopping. I like her. She said she had no idea I was still getting to know Pete, so I think I'm finally riding him better."

"That's awesome," said Tally. "I knew you guys would start to click soon."

"Thanks," said Maggie. "I'm not upset about

starting in the lower division anymore. I probably shouldn't have assumed we'd start in the two-six anyway. Thanks for talking to me about it, Tally. You're a good friend."

Tally smiled at the screen and Cam jerked her arm toward some grass that he finally found appealing. Both girls laughed. "So, how's it going there?" Maggie asked.

As Mac told her about their first show day, Tally gazed out over the sandy walking path lined with palm trees. She watched the woman at the mobile tack shop pack up for the day and two girls with their dogs laughing as they walked down the path.

Tally took a deep breath, feeling the stress from earlier float off her body.

· CHAPTER 26 ·

The next day started with turning out the horses early. Lupe and Tally took turns bringing them in and out, and giving them a good grooming afterward. The sand in the turnout went absolutely everywhere, Tally thought as she brushed some out of Maestro's forelock.

"HACK DAY," Ryan had written on the white board next to the grooming stalls. Tally liked how the board was updated each day with the plans for all of the horses.

"Morning, Tal. Morning, Lupe," said her trainer as he walked down the aisle.

"Morning," Lupe replied. "Everyone's been out already and we are wrapping up the grooming now. Mac and Isabelle are watching the pony ring and Suzette is getting breakfast."

"Great work, guys, thank you," Ryan said. "I've

been on the phone with people who have horses we can try next week. Sorry that held me up in getting here. Tally, when you're done with Maestro, why don't you tack up your horse and Sparkles so you and Mac can flat together?"

Tally grinned and said she would. There was something about that grass field that was nearly as exciting as the show ring.

Just as the sun was starting to force people out of their jackets, Tally and Mac were dressed to ride. The horses were tacked, and Lupe was completing the final step of putting earplugs in their ears.

The girls mounted and rode the short walk from the stalls to the grass field. It was enormous—easily the size of three show rings lined up side by side.

"I've got a couple more calls to make about sales so I'm here if you need me," Ryan said by the fence line. "But go ahead and hack around at will. Make sure they really stretch out their bodies at each gait."

Tally and Mac grinned at each other and set off on their own. Hacking through the big grass field was even more fun than Tally expected. She felt like a character in a book with all the scenery whizzing by as she rode, the music getting louder as she approached the short side of the field by the Grand Prix ring.

Tally's mom was always saying, "time flies when you're having fun." And that certainly applied to this Friday in Florida. Their time in the ring flew by, and after riding, it was mostly barn chores. Isabelle and Suzette pitched in, too, cleaning their tack after they rode, but the group never stopped talking and laughing. When the work was done for the day, Tally felt a little like crawling into bed, but Suzette offered to take Ryan and the girls to a restaurant on the water for dinner.

It wasn't the first time Tally had noticed people's ages slip away, but this time might have been the most memorable. Tally, Mac, Isabelle, and Suzette chatted excitedly about their horses, riding, and showing, and Ryan chimed in with some stories of his own. Dinner went by even faster than their afternoon working at the barn.

In the hotel room after dinner, Tally and Mac joked that Tally might fall asleep in the shower. Mac even tapped on the door while Tally was rinsing out her hair.

"You okay in there?" she asked. "Don't snore—you could drown!"

When Tally got in bed at nine o'clock sharp, her head had barely hit the pillow before she was fast asleep.

The alarm went off at 6:15 a.m. the next morning, and Tally was relieved to find her stomach grumbling, rather than feeling stuffed with butterflies. Talking about the pressure with Ryan had made her excited, rather than nervous, for her last couple days of showing.

When the girls arrived at the barn they went straight to the white board. No one else was on the aisle. Tally assumed they were out at the ring with Suzette.

"I want to watch the Adult Hunters, will you go with me?" Tally asked Mac.

"Sure," Mac replied. "Look at this, they moved us to Hunter 1 today."

And just like that, the butterflies came back. Tally had noticed on Thursday how much bigger everything seemed in that main hunter ring. The jumps were all built up and the tracks were all different. She'd been looking forward to having another chance to show in the "pony ring," as she'd heard people calling it.

"What's wrong?" Mac asked, sensing Tally's tension.

"Nothing, I was just hoping to get to ride in the pony ring again. I felt like I'd be more comfortable in that ring, since it would be our second day showing there."

"Well, get comfortable with being uncomfortable," Mac said with a silly grin, putting her arm around Tally. "Things are so unpredictable at a horse show."

The girls put on their boots, jackets, and helmets, to be ready before walking up to watch Suzette.

"We're looking for our older Adult Amateur Hunters now, folks," said the ring's announcer over the loudspeakers. "Adult Amateurs thirty-six and over, please make your way to Hunter Ring One."

Tally's nerves settled back down as she watched Suzette and Maestro navigate their courses. The jumps were beautiful and Tally quickly forgot about her initial preference for the pony ring. She was in Florida, after all! May as well go big and do their thing in the main hunter ring with all that made it feel special.

While Suzette's division hacked, Tally and Mac got a golf cart ride back to the stalls with Ryan. The braider was just finishing up with Cam. His braids were secured with purple yarn and one braid, about halfway down his neck, was accessorized with a little silver charm in the shape of a star. Fitting, Tally thought, because Cam *was* a star. She made a mental note to ask if she could keep the charm at the end of the show day.

Mac and Tally rode side by side up to the schooling area next to the main hunter ring. Tally had been lucky with schooling rings at horse shows up to this point. They were never particularly crowded. Until today. There were eight or nine horses in the small schooling area—Tally lost count—and one of them had a large red ribbon tied into his tail, which indicated that the horse was prone to kicking.

Warming up felt disjointed as Tally couldn't canter Cam very many strides before having to navigate her way around a horse or two.

"Come catch this middle vertical, Tal," Ryan called to her after they'd flatted in both directions. Tally turned left from the schooling area in-gate, focused on blocking Cam's right drift.

One, two, one, two, she counted...and a gray horse turned right in front of them.

"Heads up!" Ryan called, and Tally abruptly turned Cam right to avoid a head-on collision.

CHAPTER 27

"I'm so sorry," said the other rider, whose trainer was also apologizing to Ryan.

"It's okay, we all need to pay a little closer attention," Ryan replied. "Tally, call out your jump next time, okay?"

Just when she was starting to get comfortable at a big, important horse show, Tally felt totally stupid for forgetting this basic rule of the warmup area.

"Tal, come again," said Ryan, and she did her best to put her mistake out of her mind.

A few strides before making the left turn, Tally called out, "Oxer! I mean...vertical!" It was like the act of speaking turned off her brain and she forgot to keep her right leg on through the turn. Cam drifted hard to the outside and Tally lost her track entirely, finding a big chip in to the schooling jump.

"Come again. Right leg!" said Ryan.

Tally kept cantering and exhaled deeply. *The sooner you jump a good jump off both leads, the sooner you get to leave this ring.*

The next time around, she found the vertical off the right lead, and then off the left.

"I'd normally set an oxer for you next, but I think it's so packed in here you're better off just going in. That okay with you, Tal?" Ryan asked.

Tally laughed. "Yes, please!"

"Okay," he said with a grin. "Remember: There's no such thing as a perfect horse. No perfect rounds. No perfect horse shows. Perfect is a made-up thing. You have a great horse under you who can show you the ropes. It's awesome that you can ride the harder ones for me, but there's something to learn from a horse like Cam, too. You're learning how it's *supposed* to feel. Your goal is not to ride perfectly. It's to do the best you can in there to set your pace, maintain it, and stay on your track. But what's the biggest thing you need to do? The thing that's most important to me?"

"Have fun," Tally said smiling.

"Exactly," Ryan replied and then turned to the man running the in-gate. "First hunter trip, no warm-up," Ryan told him.

Tally and Cam walked through the gate and Cam looked around Hunter 1 for the first time. Ryan was right, it *was* fun to walk in not worrying about spooks or her horse sucking back. Cam seemed to love his job, and Tally loved getting to be his partner, even just for a couple of months.

"Now for a first hunter trip, we welcome back number 844, Cameron, with Tally Hart in the irons."

Tally picked up the left lead canter and broke into another genuine smile. The jumps in this ring were *so* cool, built up to look solid between the flower boxes, fuzzy green ramps, gates, and greenery. It almost didn't feel real.

As she cantered around and lined up the first few jumps, Tally noticed just how much fun she was having, taking her turn in such a gorgeous ring. Coming out of the corner to her diagonal line, she realized she had to move up. Tally put her leg on Cam, who extended his stride dramatically for the last few strides before the jump in of the line. Landing shallow, Tally kept moving him up in order to jump out in six strides. They finished their course on a five-stride line at the far end of the ring, landing to the applause of her trainer and barn friends.

CHAPTER 28

"Really good, huh, Tal?"

Tally gave Cam a pat and nodded as they exited the show ring.

"I'd say you found seven out of eight beautiful jumps, it was just too big of a move-up to the diagonal line."

"I know...but I'm actually not sure why that happened," Tally said. "Kind of a blur again."

"That's the show nerves; you understand these things much better as they happen at home. Mileage will fix that!" said Ryan. "To me, it looked like you just got comfortable riding your rhythm—like Cam suckered you into a slower canter. A little less than ring pace. Does that make sense?"

"Now I'm making a mistake that comes from being too relaxed? I kind of love that," said Tally with a laugh.

"It's all good," said Ryan, feeding Cam a peppermint from his pocket. "There's no better way for you as a rider to get comfortable than to just keep going back in the ring, again and again. And no better horse to do it on than one like this. You're here for miles."

"And smiles," Tally added.

"And smiles," Ryan agreed. "You know your next course?"

Back in the ring, Tally took her time picking up the right lead, got Cam up to ring pace, and then settled in to find their first jump.

The course went a lot like the last one, mostly smooth, but with a chip into the last line. Tally still smiled after it happened and moved up without racing to get out in five.

"Good, Tal!" said Ryan when she came out. "I don't even mind that chip so much because you corrected your mistake from the first round. Do you know why you chipped in to the last line?"

"Is it because my turn was terrible?"

"I wouldn't say terrible, but you did cut it a little bit. Probably because you got excited about having a good round, right?" asked Ryan.

"Yeah, I was just eager to get there."

"Easiest way to lose a good distance is to change your track and cut in. File that under your Florida lessons and go have fun in the hack."

After half a lap of being judged at the walk, the class trotted, tracking left.

Tally thought about keeping her post steady, and moving Cam forward in his trot with impulsion—without running him off his feet.

"Walk, please, all walk," said the announcer.

As she approached the gate, Tally squeezed her fingers and sank into her saddle. Cam transitioned smoothly down to the walk. Then something at the in-gate caught Tally's eye.

"Tal!" Ryan said in an exaggerated whisper, waving his arms to get her attention. "Keep trotting!"

Tally glanced around to see that Cam was the only horse out of the dozen or so in the ring that was walking. She gave him a swift thump with both legs and he stepped into his left lead canter. Tally hastily brought him back down to the trot.

She'd been listening to the announcer from the *pony* ring—the one she'd hoped to stay in that day.

There was nothing to do but laugh to herself. Ryan said she'd rack up the lessons in Florida, and that was exactly what she was doing.

As the horses all lined up at the end of the class, Tally figured she wouldn't get a ribbon, but that was okay. She had used the class to practice getting Cam seen, and keeping him seen, even when the ring was busy. While waiting for the class to be pinned, she subtly counted the horses. Fourteen total. It had been great practice for hacking Cam in such good company.

"First place and congratulations goes to number 365, RDK Snow Owl, and Alegra Rudnick. Second place is number 844, Cameron, and Tally Hart."

Tally's jaw dropped open for a moment before she regained her composure, giving Cam a pat and riding out of the line for her ribbon. Ryan was in the schooling ring with Mac but he gave her a thumbs-up. Either the judge didn't see her mistake, or she considered it a forgivable one, Tally thought.

"You can ride him back down to the barn, Tal," said Lupe. "You want the ribbon on his bridle? Show everyone what a great horse you have?"

Tally beamed and nodded her head yes. Cam seemed as happy to have a ribbon attached to his bridle as she was. They took a long, meandering route home, their red ribbon fluttering in the breeze.

CHAPTER 29

"I can't believe it's our last day already." Mac scrunched her face into a frown as she and Tally watched Suzette and Maestro warming up on Sunday morning. "Why did it go so fast?"

"Because we were having fun?" suggested Tally. She pointed to the two-stride in the middle of the ring. "Are we going to have that in my division?" Tally asked.

Mac shook her head no. "I've never seen a two-stride in a two-foot-six division. But if they do leave it, you'll love it."

"People talk about two-strides being so hard," Tally said.

"It's rough if you get in badly, because then you could add a third stride and have that big chip to get out. But I try to think of it like a two-stride *line*, and that keeps me from over-analyzing it," Mac said with a shrug. "That's really what it is, after all. A very short line."

"You know you're brilliant sometimes?" said Tally. Mac elbowed her playfully in the arm.

Hunter Ring One started out with a derby on Sundays and the girls whooped and cheered for Suzette's first round, which scored an 83—almost certain to bring her back in the top 12 for the handy round. Tally and Mac watched all of the horses in the first round, calculating that Suzette and Maestro were fourth going into the handy.

"Hey girls," said Isabelle, who'd joined them in the bleachers. "Ryan wants you two to walk down and get dressed. He says this ring is going to move faster than yesterday since there are no under saddle classes."

"Are you sure we don't have time to stay and watch Suzette's second round?" asked Mac.

Isabelle glanced out over the ring and then back at the girls. "Considering that they haven't started the handy...and the fact that it's *Ryan*...I would suggest that you go get your boots and helmets on."

Tally laughed. "Come on, let's walk down. I'm going to grab an orange juice on the way."

♘

The only thing that Tally was even slightly nervous about for her final show day in Florida was the schooling ring. Whatever happened in the show ring would be okay. But dodging other horses as she approached a single jump just four strides from the short side was no fun at all.

"Why do you look so cool and relaxed when you warm up?" Tally asked Mac as they rode side by side from the stalls to the ring.

"I do?" Mac asked. "I hate the schooling ring. I think everyone does. But I've heard Ryan describe it as preparing the horses for what they're going to be doing in the show ring, so I try to think of it that way. Like I'm doing my job to properly prepare Sparkles. And also, the quicker I can get my job done in there, the quicker I can get out."

"I had exactly that same thought yesterday!" said Tally as Cam slowed down to eye a motorized scooter parked by the mobile tack shop. He stopped next to it to get a better look. Tally took the opportunity to gaze at his perfect braids, secured with blue yarn this time.

"Never seen one of those before, huh, buddy?" Mac asked as Cam breathed on the scooter noisily.

He reminded Tally of a dragon. Then he turned away from it and kept walking toward the show ring.

The schooling ring was a zoo again, but Tally stayed focused on the task at hand. When she jumped her warm-up fence off the left lead, she was sure to block Cam's right drift *and* call for her jump before making the turn.

"Atta girl, Tal, now come jump it off the right," said Ryan. "Lupe, could you put Mac in the first rotation over in the pony ring, please? Tally, remember to call for your jump again."

Tally found a tight distance the first time, and then came around again with a better turn and jumped out of a nice, medium spot.

"You good?" Ryan asked.

"Good," said Tally with a firm nod.

"You know the drill. Have fun, maintain your rhythm, hold your track out of the left turns. Oh, and did I say to have fun?"

Tally's last two courses of her division felt like a dream. She had little things here and there that could have been better—she still needed to work on smoothly moving Cam up to jump from the gap, rather than putting her leg on so hard that he surged forward. But for the most part, both trips felt really solid, and Ryan said they were her best in Florida.

They took their time going over her final course, a classic round that featured a roll-back and a bending line. Ryan explained that after jumping in to the judge's line, all Tally had to do was turn her head left to indicate to Cam that he wouldn't be jumping the oxer out.

"That will shift your weight enough to tell the horse that he's going to turn," Ryan explained. "Make sure you land and canter away for three strides before you actually make that left turn and then shape it as you bend back to the single oxer. It's not about getting there fast, it's about being efficient. Then ride the oxer off your eye. Have fun and enjoy it," he added with a smile.

Tally's first five jumps all came up nicely and she reminded herself about riding away for three strides after she jumped into the judge's line. She turned her head upon landing and kept both legs on to ride Cam straight—he did feel her shift her weight and would have happily fallen in sooner to turn, but Tally stuck to her plan. They turned left, Tally kept her right leg on

Cam to keep him straight, and just like that, they were just a few strides away from the oxer.

One, two, one, two, she counted, and the oxer came right up out of stride.

You couldn't have paid Tally to *stop* smiling as they headed for their final line heading home. She moved Cam up smoothly (finally!) to just a slightly gappy distance jumping in to the line, and then focused her eyes on the oxer on the bend, rather than the oxer out of the regular five-stride line from their last two courses.

Cam was right there with her, sighting in on that last jump with Tally.

Was it six or seven strides? Tally wondered. She'd been so focused on the rollback that she was now blanking on the related distance in her last line.

Two, three, four, five—okay, it's seven!—six, seven, she whispered, resisting the urge to lay on Cam's neck as they jumped out. Something about finding a perfect distance out of stride always made her want to do that, but Tally made sure to control her body as Cam made a lofty, round effort over their final fence in the classic.

⋃

"The score for Cameron and Tally Hart is an 82, making their two-round classic score a 162," said the announcer. Ryan clapped loudly at the in-gate.

"Well-done, Tally," he said, giving Cam a pat and a peppermint as he stepped out of the ring. "You can check Florida off the list of places you've shown successfully."

CHAPTER 30

Tally felt like she was floating on air as she hugged Cam outside the schooling area. Lupe offered to walk Cam back to the stalls so Tally could watch her friend compete. Tally thanked him, then walked over to the pony ring and took videos for Mac, who nailed her own two courses and classic round.

The girls celebrated with ice cream bars from the food stand on their way back to the stalls. It was time to pack up their trunks before the flight home.

"You know how you did?" Lupe asked them.

"No, we both went early in our divisions and there were a lot in there," said Mac.

"I'll ask Ryan to check for your ribbons after he wraps up with Isabelle. You are taking a car service to the airport?" he asked.

"Yes, my mom set it up," said Mac. "I just got a text from the driver that he's ten minutes away."

Tally grabbed a pair of long carrots from the bucket by the tack trunks and let herself into Cam's stall for one last snuggle.

"Thanks for teaching me how to show in Florida, buddy," she said, leaning into his chest and stroking both sides of his neck while he noisily chewed the carrots. "I love you. Have fun rolling around in the sand turnout next week."

"Will Ryan ride the horses next week, Mac?" Tally asked her friend, who was in the next stall saying goodbye to Sparkles.

"Yup, he will give them tomorrow off and then probably hack them every day until the horses ship home."

"I think I do want to be a trainer when I grow up," said Tally. Cam nickered, seemingly in agreement.

"Right? I know it's hard work but getting to ride so many horses, literally every day...what else is there?" said Mac. "Let's go into business together after college."

"Deal," said Tally with a grin.

U

"Car's here!" Lupe called from the end of the aisle. "Ryan will bring your ribbons home next week. You girls better get going."

Tally and Mac thanked him for all of his help and Mac handed him an envelope. "From my mom and Tally's mom," she said.

"*Gracias*," said Lupe. "And congratulations on your great rides."

In the car on the way to the airport, the girls were mostly quiet, lost in thoughts of their busy week at the horse show. Tally wondered how much more time she'd have with Cam before Pia returned home, but made herself focus instead on what a special, magical few days she'd had showing her sweet packer in a beautiful setting with great competition.

When the car pulled up to the airport, the driver informed them that their parents had taken care of the fare, as well as the tip, and reminded them that they should check in with the agent at their gate since they were traveling alone.

Tally followed Mac inside the terminal, feeling sad to leave Florida but excited to sleep in her own bed and to see her mom and dad. Her phone chimed, but Tally left it in her pocket until they were through security and headed for their gate.

When they arrived, Mac and Tally checked in with the gate agent and then sat down. That's when Tally remembered the notification from her phone. She fished it out of her pocket to find a photo from Ryan.

Laid out on her tack trunk were four ribbons—one white, two blue, and a Reserve Champion tricolor.

Catch up on the
SHOW STRIDES series!

School Horses and Show Ponies

Confidence Comeback

Moving Up and Moving On

Testing Friendships

Always available at **theplaidhorse.com**

ABOUT THE AUTHORS

 **Piper Klemm, Ph.D.** is the publisher of *The Plaid Horse* magazine. She co-hosts the weekly podcast of The Plaid Horse, the #Plaidcast, and is a college professor. She has been riding since she was eight years old and currently owns several hunter ponies who compete on the horse show circuit. She frequently competes in the Adult Amateurs across North America on her horse of a lifetime, MTM Sandwich, so you might see her at a horse show near you!

FIND HER ONLINE AT piper-klemm.com
@piperklemm

 Rennie Dyball has loved horses for as long as she can remember. She began taking lessons at age twelve, was captain of the Penn State equestrian team, and now shows in the Low Adult hunters. Rennie spent fifteen years as a writer and editor at *People* and has co-authored more than a dozen books. Her picture book debut, *B Is for Bellies,* will be published by Clarion in 2023. With *Show Strides,* Rennie is delighted to combine two of her greatest passions—writing and riding.

FIND HER ONLINE AT renniedyball.com
@renniedyball

WHO'S WHO
IN *SHOW STRIDES*?

Ava Foster: Friends with Tally and Kaitlyn, used to own Danny but quit riding to pursue gymnastics

Beau: Field Ridge pony who belongs to a rider named Marion

Brenna: Barn manager at Quince Oaks

Carlo: Jacob's horse, a jumper

Cindy Bennett: Mac's mom

Copper Top Farm: Show facility on the Gulf Coast of Florida

Field Day: (a.k.a. Pete) Maggie's new horse

Field Ridge: Ryan's business within Quince Oaks

Gelati: A school pony at Quince Oaks

Goose: A green pony that Tally catch-rode

Isabelle: A junior rider who trains with Ryan and has a horse named Pip

Jacob Viston: A junior rider who trains with Ryan

James Hart: Tally's dad

Jordan: Takes lessons at Quince Oaks, sometimes with Tally

Kaitlyn Rowe: Tally's friend at school

Kelsey: Working student for the riding school

Lil Bit: A school pony at Quince Oaks

Lupe: Field Ridge's head groom

Mackenzie (Mac) Bennett: Junior rider who owns Joey and Sparklepants and competes in the pony hunter divisions

Maestro: Suzette's horse, who competes in the Adult Amateur Hunters

Maggie Edwards: Junior rider who trains with Ryan

Marsha: The barn secretary at Quince Oaks

Meg: Tally's instructor at Quince Oaks before Ryan

Nicole: A new instructor at Quince Oaks

Obie: Tally's project horse who gets leased to another student of Ryan's

Olivia Motes: A rider who bought Goose after trying him at Pony Finals

Pia: Cameron's owner who shows in the Adult Amateur Hunters

Pip: Isabelle's junior hunter

Quince Oaks: The barn

Ryan McNeil: The Field Ridge trainer who operates out of Quince Oaks

Scout: One of the Quince Oaks school horses

Smoke Hill Jet Set (a.k.a. Joey): Mac's medium pony hunter

Stacy Hart: Tally's mom

Sparklepants: Mac's new large pony, a.k.a. Sparkles

Stonelea Dance Party (a.k.a. Danny): Formerly Ava Foster's pony, sold through Ryan

Suzette: An adult amateur who rides with Ryan

U

Sweet Talker (a.k.a. Sweetie): Tally's favorite school horse

Tally Hart: Rides in the lesson program and Ryan's sales ponies at Quince Oaks

Toots: One of the school ponies

GLOSSARY OF HORSE TERMINOLOGY

A circuit: Nationally-rated horse shows.

backed: When a horse or pony that's newly in training has a rider on its back for the first time.

base: Where a horse or pony leaves the ground in front of a jump; also: refers to the rider's feet in the stirrups, with heels down acting as anchors, or a base of support, for the rider's legs.

bay: A horse color that consists of a brown coat and black points (black mane, tail, ear edges, and legs).

buzzer: The sound in the jumper ring that indicates a horse and rider have forty-five seconds to cross the timers in front of the first jump.

canter: A three-beat gait that horses and ponies travel in—it's a more controlled version of the gallop, the fastest of the gaits (walk, trot, canter, gallop).

catch-riding: When a rider gets to ride and/or show a horse or pony owned by someone else.

cavaletti: Very small jumps for schooling or jumping practice.

chestnut: A reddish brown horse/pony coat color, with a lighter mane and tail.

chip: When a horse or pony takes off too close to a jump by adding in an extra stride near the base.

colic: A catch-all term for gastrointestinal distress in a horse or pony; can be fatal in severe cases.

colt: A young male horse.

conformation class: A horse show class in which the animals are modeled and judged on their build.

crest release: When the rider places his or her hands up the horse or pony's neck, thus adding slack to the reins and giving the animal freedom of movement in its head and neck.

crop/bat: A small (and humane!) whip that is used behind the rider's leg when the rider's leg aid is not sufficient.

cross-rail: A jump with two rails that form an X.

currycomb: A grooming tool used in circles on a horse or pony's coat to lift out dirt.

Devon: An annual, prestigious invitation-only horse show in Pennsylvania.

diagonal line: Two jumps with a set distance between them set on the diagonal of a riding ring.

distance: The take-off spot for a jump. Riders often talk about "finding distances," which means finding the ideal spot to take off over a jump.

flower boxes: Jump adornments that are placed below the lowest rail of a jump.

gate: Part of a jump that is placed in the jump cups instead of a rail. Typically heavier than a standard jump rail so horses and ponies can be more careful in jumping them so as not to hit a hoof.

gelding: A castrated male horse.

girth: A piece of equipment that holds the saddle securely on a horse or pony. The girth attaches to the billets under the flaps of the saddle and goes underneath the horse, behind the front legs, and is secured on the billets on the other side.

green: A horse or pony who has less training and/or experience (the opposite of a "made" horse or pony, which has lots of training and experience).

gymnastic: A line of jumps with one, two, or zero strides between them (no strides in between jumps is called a bounce—the horse or pony lands off the first jump and immediately takes off for the next without taking a stride).

hack: Can either mean riding a horse on the flat (no jumps) in an indoor ring or outside; or, an under saddle class at a horse show, in which the animal is judged on its performance on the flat.

hands: A unit of measurement for horse or pony heights. One hand equals 4 inches, so a 15-hand horse is 60 inches tall from the ground to its withers. A pony that's 12.2 hands is 12 hands, 2 inches, or 50 inches tall at the withers.

handy: A handy class in a hunter division is meant to test a horse or pony's handiness, or its ability to navigate a course. Special elements included in handy hunter courses may include trot jumps, roll backs, and hand gallops.

in-and-out: Two jumps with one stride in between, typically part of a jumper or equitation course.

in-gate: Sometimes just referred to as "the gate," it's where horses enter and exit the show ring. Usually it's one gate for both directions; sometimes two gates will be in use, one to go in and the other to come out.

jog: How ponies and horses in A-rated divisions finish each over fences class; the judge calls them to jog across the ring to check for soundness and orders the class. During the COVID-19 pandemic, the closing circle trot was used in place of the jog.

jump-off: An element in many jumper classes in which horses and riders jump a shortened course, and the fastest time with the fewest jumping and time faults wins.

large pony: A pony that measures over 13.2 hands, but no taller than 14.2 hands.

lead changes: Changing of the canter lead from right to left or vice versa. The inside front and hind legs stretch farther when the horse or pony is on the correct lead. A lead change can be executed in two ways: A simple lead change is when the horse transitions from the canter to the trot and then picks up the opposite canter lead. In a flying lead change, the horse changes their lead in midair without trotting.

line: Two jumps with a set number of strides between them.

longe line: A long lead that attaches to a horse's halter or bridle. The horse or pony travels around the handler in a large circle to work on the flat with commands from the handler holding the line.

Low Children's Hunter and Low Adult Amateur Hunter: Horse show divisions where the fences are 2'6"

Maclay: One of the big equitation or "big eq" classes for junior riders. Riders compete in regional Maclay classes to qualify for the annual Maclay Final. The final is currently held at the National Horse Show at the Kentucky Horse Park in the fall.

mare: A mature female horse.

martingale: A piece of tack intended to keep a horse or pony from raising its head too high. The martingale attaches to the girth, between the animal's front legs, and then (in a standing martingale) a single strap attaches to the noseband or (in a running martingale) a pair of straps attach to the reins.

medium pony: A pony taller than 12.2 hands, but no taller than 13.2 hands.

outside line: A line of jumps with a set number of strides between them set on the long sides of the riding ring. An outside line set on the same side of the ring as the judge's box/stand is called a judge's line.

oxer: A type of jump that features two sets of standards and two top rails, which can be set even (called a square oxer) or uneven, with the back rail higher than the front. A typical hunter over fences class features single oxers as well as oxers set as the "out" jump in lines.

packer: An expression that describes a very experienced horse or pony that can "pack" their rider around the show ring.

palomino: A horse or pony with a golden color coat and a white mane and tail.

pinned: The way a horse show class is ordered and ribbons are awarded, typically from first through sixth or first through eighth place (though some classes go to tenth or even twentieth place).

polos: Also called polo wraps, they provide protection and support to a horse or pony's legs while being ridden.

pommel: The front part of an English saddle; the rider sits behind this.

Pony Finals: An annual show, currently held at the Kentucky Horse Park, in which ponies who were champion or reserve at an A-rated show are eligible to compete.

posting trot: When a rider posts (stands up and sits down in the saddle) as the horse or pony is trotting, making the gait more comfortable and less bouncy for both the rider and the animal.

quarter sheet: A blanket intended for cold weather riding that attaches under the saddle flaps and loops under the horse or pony's tail.

regular pony hunter division (sometimes called "the division"): A national or A-rated horse show division in which small ponies jump 2'3", medium ponies jump 2'6", and large ponies jump 2'9"–3'.

rein: The reins are part of the bridle and attach to the horse or pony's bit. Used for steering and slowing down.

sales pony/sales horse: A pony or horse that is offered for sale; trainers often market a sales horse or pony through ads and by showing the animal.

school horses/school ponies: Horses or ponies who are used in a program teaching riding lessons.

schooling ring: A ring at a horse show designated for warming up or schooling.

schooling shows: Unrated shows intended for practice as well as for green horses and ponies to gain experience.

shadbelly: A formal show coat with tails typically worn for hunter classics and derbies.

small pony: A pony that measures 12.2 hands and under.

spooky: A horse or pony that's acting easily spooked or startled.

spurs: An artificial aid, worn on a rider's boots to add impulsion.

stakes class: Part of a hunter division; it's a class that offers prize money.

stirrup irons: The metal loops in which riders place their feet.

stirrup leathers: Threaded through the stirrup bars of the saddle and through the stirrups themselves; the leathers hold the stirrups in place.

swap: When a horse or pony unnecessarily changes its lead on course.

tack: The equipment a horse wears to be ridden (e.g. saddle, bridle, martingale).

tall boots: The knee-high, black leather boots that hunter/jumper/equitation riders wear with breeches when they reach a certain height or age. Prior to that, riders wear paddock boots (which only reach past the ankles) and jodhpurs with garter straps.

ticketed schooling: Opportunities offered by some horse shows to ride in show rings unjudged, as practice for horses and riders.

trail rides: A ride that takes place out on trails instead of in a riding ring.

transition: When a horse or pony moves from one gait to another. For example, moving from the canter to the trot is a downward transition; moving from the walk to the trot is an upward transition.

trot: A two-beat gait in which the horse or pony's legs move in diagonal pairs.

tricolors: The ribbons awarded for champion (most points in a division) and reserve champion (second highest number of points in that division).

trip: Another term for a jumping round, or course, mostly used at shows, as in, "the pony's first trip."

vertical: A jump that includes one set of standards and a rail or rails set horizontally.

THE PLAID HORSE

ENCOURAGES EVERY EQUESTRIAN TO:

READ   *The Plaid Horse* magazine
In print and online at
theplaidhorse.com/read

Subscribe at **theplaidhorse.com/subscribe**

READ   *With Purpose: The Balmoral Standard*
by Carleton Brooks and Traci Brooks
with Rennie Dyball

Available at **theplaidhorse.com/books**

READ   The re-release of
*Geoff Teall on Riding Hunters, Jumpers and
Equitation: Develop a Winning Style*

Available at **theplaidhorse.com/books**

LEARN   Explore your college credit
education opportunities at
theplaidhorse.com/college

LISTEN   The #Plaidcast
The podcast of *The Plaid Horse* at
theplaidhorse.com/listen

On Audible, Apple Podcasts, Google Play,
Stitcher, and Spotify

ENGAGE   Find out about local events
featuring Piper & Rennie at
theplaidhorse.com

FOLLOW   *The Plaid Horse* on social media:

Facebook.com/theplaidhorsemag

Twitter @PlaidHorsemag

Instagram @theplaidhorsemag

Pinterest @theplaidhorsemag

NORTH AMERICA'S HORSE SHOW MAGAZINE • PUBLISHED SINCE 2003

Available at **theplaidhorse.com/books**

WITH PURPOSE: THE BALMORAL STANDARD

By Traci Brooks and Carleton Brooks with Rennie Dyball

CHAPTER 3:
Think Like a Horse

No one *really* knows what horses are thinking. If we did, it would make our jobs a whole lot easier. However, after several decades of working with horses, based on our experience and how horses react to us, we have some pretty good ideas.

Many a horseman have wondered what makes a performance horse happy, and from what we can tell, having a routine is paramount. And with a routine comes expectations. A show horse—and any horse, really, that has a job working with humans—has expectations placed on them. Understanding those expectations and knowing what's coming throughout their day seems to go a long way with a horse. Changing the routine can be jarring, and mixed messages about our expectations are confusing. So, to the best of our ability, we maintain a consistent routine and try to "speak horse" so the animals know what to expect.

> *"Our motto is routine, structure, expectation, positivity." —TB*

Horses don't like surprises. Most of them don't like things happening too fast. Positive energy and feedback are important. So is physical comfort—the horse's *body* should feel good. If you're walking around and your knees hurt or your back hurts, you're not going to feel like you can perform at your best. We try to read the horses and take care of their physical comfort.

As previously mentioned, we aren't big on treats in our barns, but we understand that humans want to know how to best reward their horse for a job well done. Horses work hard for us and expect nothing in return, so it's human nature to want to acknowledge their efforts. To reward them, we suggest focusing on attention and positive reinforcement.

U

"You'll notice I never pet a horse. I stroke them.
If you're going to tap a horse with a stick, isn't a
hard pat the same thing? If you rub your horse,
it's comforting. Think about how a pat versus a
rub would feel to you." —CB

We believe that if a horse thinks you are part of his herd, he will go along with you. There is a survival instinct at play, too—some horses might translate doing their job into getting fed. A lot of horses are very motivated by the reward that comes with doing their job, even if that reward is as simple as getting hay and water, kindness and attention.

Some horses enjoy their jobs more than others. People tend to say things like "that one loves its job," or "this horse loves to be at a show." How much truth is there to that? We believe that horses are individuals and should be treated as such.

We have one horse who is over twenty years old, and if you retired him and put him in a field, he would not do well. He needs to have a job and he needs to get brushed every day. Even if someone just takes him out, grooms him, gives him affection, and jumps a few jumps now and then, he is happy. Horses like him need the interaction because that is all they know. Each horse is an individual as much as humans are. Some simply want to work more than others. Show horses are so domesticated that many lose a lot of their wildness and flight instinct, so what they're left with is their job and the human interaction that comes with it.

"When my junior hunter got older and stopped horse showing, I could not turn her out. She would walk maybe fifteen feet away to graze, but she did not know anything but me and I had spent so much time with her. So, we ended up making her a school horse. One year, we didn't know that she was in foal. She never stopped teaching lessons, and two weeks after having the baby, she was teaching lessons again. She loved it. We tried to leave her just with the foal but she would stand by the gate and stare at the ring. So we finally put her in a pen with her foal and she did not ever mind leaving to teach a lesson or two. She gave us this look that said, 'I am good to go.' Some of these horses, that is just what they know." —CB

You can tell when show horses are eager to perform. We have a few who are a little blah about being ridden on the flat, but then you point them at the jumps and they become so much more engaged. It's all about the individual personalities and we try to work that into each horse's care and training program.

When something is important to you, the human, the horses can feel the difference. And when they go someplace new, or someplace really different from what they're used to, like Indoors, it's an entirely new routine. They are getting all this attention and you are feeling intense, so they're going to feel that. They can feel when it's important. Special horses rise to the occasion.

"I have always taken pride in listening to the horse and treating each horse as an individual, and I remember them all for their unique traits that led them to become such stars in the show ring." —CB

SPEAKING HORSE

Horses perform at their best when they feel content, comfortable, and safe. As such, we are constantly assessing, to the best of our ability, what their behavior and body language are telling us. We think when the vibe of the entire team is relaxed, confident, and happy, the horses feel that and follow suit. If the atmosphere is tense, the horses pick up on that, too.

There are lots of ways to create a relaxed, confident, and happy atmosphere in your stable. Some people play music in their stable to create that type of atmosphere. But it mainly comes down to the people who work there, and the attitudes they bring with them. The horses will generally read that and react to it or mirror it.

"When I hang out with the horses I sometimes let them breathe on me (they like our necks!) and I put my nose by theirs and breathe into their nostrils. And when they breathe back, you can feel them relax. We also like to rub a horse near the withers because that's where horses nuzzle each other." —TB

There are subtle but translatable behaviors you can watch for, like when a horse opens their nostrils wide, sometimes paired with lifting their head and holding their breath. That means they're sensing something in the distance. It could be from an observational viewpoint or a defensive viewpoint. Horses are flight animals, so if they think there's something in the distance, they will raise their head slightly and open their nostrils to allow their senses to work. That doesn't mean there's anything wrong. But many people grab their horse or worry about a spook coming, instead of just allowing the process to happen. Try not to be (over) reactive. Sometimes you've got to let a horse go through the process. They do it all day long and most people don't notice. You may get on in the warmup ring and your horse looks down to the next warmup ring, raising his head and opening his nostrils, because there's a horse down there panicked by something. Your horse might observe that, and the best thing you can do is let them go through that process while you act *as if* you're relaxed (even if you're not). Do not let it escalate.

Another behavior that people tend to notice is yawning. It's a way for horses to relieve their muscles, first off, just like when we yawn. In fact, yawning is really an exaggeration of taking a deep breath. It's a sign of being relaxed. Think of this as a positive!

♘

When a horse cocks their ear back, (possibly with their eye looking behind them), they're listening to you.

There are behaviors with the horse's tail that you can interpret as well. The underside of the tail is a very sensitive part of the horse's body. Clamping the tail down indicates distress or anger. If a horse swishes his tail in a relaxed manner, that means his body is loose and he's willing to do something. At times, the tail will also move as you close your leg—toward the side where you are adding pressure. A horse uses his tail for balance, so a fair amount of movement is to be expected. But lots of swishing of the tail can indicate a clashing of aids, or a form of discomfort or annoyance.

A lot of interpreting horse behaviors comes down to intuition. You have to be 100 percent present to really feel what your horse is feeling. And always putting yourself in your horse's shoes.

"We had a horse on trial for an adult, and we didn't know the horse very well. I was holding the horse for the rider at the mounting block, and I could just feel that the horse was anxious. I could feel him holding his breath and getting

a little tense. As the rider swung her leg over, I could feel that the horse wasn't relaxed and it had some pent-up energy. The rider had only walked a little loop, and I told her to get off. She was confused, but she did. (Riders have to listen to their trainers, immediately and without question, to stay safe. Hesitation can be dangerous.) We took the horse over to the turnout and I told the rider I thought the horse needed to buck. We turned him out and he ran around, bucked three or four times, and came walking over to us as if to say, 'I'm done, thank you. Now we can proceed.' The rider got back on and the horse was perfect. The horse wasn't being bad before, he just needed to get some extra energy out. It was a cool Tuesday morning and the horse just needed a moment. We gave him a moment and then he was fine." —TB

People ask us all the time, "*How* do you learn to speak horse?" "How do you know what's about to happen?" If you're paying attention and trying to understand the animals—and you're truly focused and not distracted or on your phone—you pick up on this stuff over time. You won't always be right, but you start to get the idea of what horses are trying to tell you. A lot of times, it's simply imagining what something feels like to a horse in order to "speak" their language, putting yourself in their position, and "being" the horse.

In another example, we had one horse that was coughing a bit and we put him on cough medicine and tried wetting his hay. We thought maybe it was allergies. Then we tried making the noseband really loose, so that horse could open its mouth a little more and move his tongue—allowing him to swallow and breathe. And that was when he stopped coughing. It's all about putting yourself in that horse's position.

"Horses are always trying to tell us something. Our job is to always be listening and trying to understand them." —TB

Your horse is also in tune to your breathing. This is another place to act *as if* you're relaxed, even if you're not. When you hold your breath, so does your horse. When your breath is shallow, your horse's is too.

U

When we hear a horse take a deep breath, we automatically relax and feel grateful to know that the horse has relaxed, too. They have to be relaxed to perform their best. To us, that is a sign of a happy and content horse, whether you are riding or just working in the barn. A deep breath from a horse tells you that they are comfortable and understand what is being asked of them. It's not that different from people!

If you want your horse to take a deep breath, remember that they will often mimic you. So if you take a deep breath in and then let it all out slowly, know that your horse will also relax. We use this on course and we build it into our course plan—where will we take a breath? After jump four? If you do a big, *slow* exhale on course, be ready to back it up with some leg because a lot of times the horses will almost stop! To them, it may feel like you're at the end of your course or exercise, and you're about to relax into a walk—but instead you want them to continue on after that moment of relaxation. It's a reset. A pause. Use it as a tool.

Oftentimes with novice or less experienced riders, we teach them to slow or stop their horses only from adjusting their breath (along with their weight). No other aids. They are always in awe when they feel how well it works!

It's always nice to see when a horse wants to be around you. We don't ever want our horses to be afraid of us. We try to win them over. Once we do, being with us is the horse's comfort. When a horse follows you, that's a great sign that he trusts you in his space.

"I try to sense what the horse is feeling and put myself in their situation so I can feel it." —CB

Look for
**SHOW STRIDES
BOOK 6**
in 2023!